CW01081908

VISIT BRITAIN'S
SEASIDE PIERS

A HERITAGE HUNTER GUIDE

A guidebook and logbook for visiting 61 piers
in England, Wales and Scotland

More books in this series and a free history newsletter:
www.heritagehunter.co.uk

CONTENTS

INTRODUCTION

A pier is an elevated structure that extends over and above a body of water, typically projecting outward from the shoreline. It is usually supported by a series of piles or pillars, providing access to offshore areas without getting wet. Piers around the world serve a variety of purposes, including fishing, boat docking for passengers and cargo, and seaside recreation. In addition to these common uses, architectural piers can also support bridges, buildings and walkways, demonstrating their versatile nature.

The open structure of piers allows tides and currents to flow with minimal obstruction, in contrast to the solid foundations of quays or the closely spaced piles of wharfs. These more substantial structures can act as breakwaters and are more prone to silting. Piers can differ greatly in size and complexity, from simple lightweight wooden structures to massive constructions extending over 1,600 metres (5,200 feet) in length. In Europe, the term typically evokes images of Victorian cast iron pleasure piers, even though piers have a history that predates the Victorian era.

Piers can be categorized according to their primary purpose, although there is frequently overlap between the categories. Pleasure piers, for example, might not only serve as recreational spaces but also accommodate pleasure steamers and other similar vessels. Conversely, working piers can transition to leisure use when rendered obsolete by advancements in cargo-handling technology. Many piers around the world are of the floating variety, which enables them to rise and fall with the tide along with the boats tied to them. This design prevents damage to boats from overly taut or loose tie-lines caused by changing tides.

Seaside pleasure piers, which first emerged in Britain during the early 19th century, have an interesting history. Among the earliest structures were Ryde Pier, built in 1813/4; Trinity Chain Pier near Leith, constructed in 1821; and Brighton Chain Pier, completed in 1823. At that time, the introduction of steamships and railways allowed for the first instances of mass tourism to dedicated seaside resorts. Due to the large tidal ranges at many of these resorts, passengers arriving by pleasure steamer could use a pier to disembark safely. Furthermore, the pleasure pier allowed holidaymakers to stroll over and alongside the sea at all times, even when the sea was not visible from the shore.

The golden age of pier-building spanned from the early 19th to the early 20th century. Out of the 89 piers that were built in England and Wales between 1814 and 1910, however, only 50 are still standing.

The world's longest pleasure pier is located at Southend-on-Sea, Essex, and extends 1.3 miles (2.1 km) into the Thames Estuary. Pleasure piers often incorporate amusements and theatres as part of their attractions, providing a comprehensive entertainment experience. These piers can be unroofed, completely enclosed, or partially open and partially closed. Initially, pleasure piers were constructed primarily from wood, with the first iron pleasure pier, Margate Jetty, opening in 1855.

As mentioned above, the first documented pier in England, Ryde Pier, opened in 1814 on the Isle of Wight as a landing stage for ferries to and from the mainland. While it also served as a leisure destination in the past, it is still used for its original purpose today. Gravesend Town Pier in Kent, which opened in 1834, is the oldest cast iron pier in the world. Piers became increasingly fashionable at seaside resorts in England and Wales during the Victorian era, peaking in the 1860s with 22 piers built during that decade.

A quintessential symbol of the British seaside holiday, more than 100 pleasure piers were established along the UK coast by 1914. Many of these piers are regarded as prime examples of Victorian architecture, with a significant number of architecturally noteworthy piers still standing today. Unfortunately, some of these iconic structures have been lost over time, including two piers at Brighton in East Sussex, one at New Brighton in the

Wirral, and three at Blackpool in Lancashire. Two piers, Brighton's now-derelict West Pier and Clevedon Pier, have been designated as Grade 1 listed structures, highlighting their architectural and historical significance.

The Birnbeck Pier in Weston-super-Mare holds a unique distinction as the only pier in the world connected to an island. This remarkable feature adds to the charm and allure of this extraordinary structure.

The enduring popularity of piers as leisure destinations can be attributed to their ability to offer a variety of entertainment options, from amusement rides and games to theatrical performances and dining establishments. In addition, their picturesque locations often provide stunning panoramic views of the surrounding coastline, making them a favourite among tourists and locals alike.

A NOTE ON THIS GUIDE

This book lists all 61 seaside piers standing across the UK – it includes those on larger estuaries such as those of the Severn and the Thames, but not the many small piers and jetties alng the Thames within London, for example. Information on places to visit, eat and drink was compiled in 2023 and may be subject to change.

🏛 – English Heritage property

🏰 – National Trust/National Trust for Scotland property

PIERS IN ENGLAND

Blackpool: Central Pier

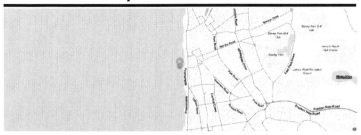

Promenade, FY1 5BB • www.centralpierblackpool.co.uk

Central Pier is one of the three piers in Blackpool, located between the other two. Central Pier opened on 30 May 1868, and at that time, it was 503 yards in length. The landing jetty was 131 yards long and was used at low tide. Dancing facilities provided the early fun, but in the 20th century, roller skating, fairground rides and amusement machines were introduced. Steamboat excursions departed from the landing jetty as they did from North Pier. After the Second World War, the dance halls became less popular, and the facilities were converted into a theatre, bars, and amusement arcades by the 1970s. In 1986, the pierhead theatre was modernized and became known as 'Peggy Sue's Showboat', and in 1990, a 33-metre-high (108 ft) Ferris wheel was erected, which was a half-scale reference to the Victorian attraction that had been part of the Winter Gardens complex a century earlier. The pier caught fire in July 2020, destroying a fairground ride and damaging an engineering shed halfway along the pier.

Nearby pubs: Pirates Bay Family Bar, Promenade; Uncle Peter Websters, 123 Promenade; Gaietys Karaoke Bar, 169 Promenade

Nearby cafes: Wheelhouse Cafe, Promenade; Yorkshire Street Grill, 167 Promenade; Chiccos Cafe, Chapel Street

Nearby car parks: Pier Street Car Park, Pier Street; York Street Car Park, York Street; Bonny Street, Foxhall

Nearest bus stop: Bank Hey Street, Foxhall

Nearest station: Blackpool North, Talbot Road

Nearby places to visit: Blackpool Tower; Blackpool Illuminations; Golden Mile; North Pier; South Pier

❏ **Date visited:**
Notes on visit:

Blackpool: North Pier

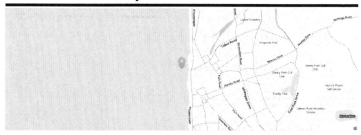

Promenade, FY1 1NE • blackpoolpiers.co.uk

North Pier is the oldest and longest of the three in Blackpool. Initially intended as a promenade, it expanded its attractions to include theatres and bars due to competition. Catering to a higher-class market, North Pier offered orchestra concerts and respectable comedians, unlike the other piers that attracted working-class patrons with open-air dancing and amusements. As a Grade II listed building, designated by English Heritage, it is the oldest surviving pier created by Eugenius Birch. Despite damage from fires, storms, and boat collisions, the pier remains in regular use, featuring bars, a theatre, a carousel and an arcade. Construction of Blackpool Pier (later North Pier) began in May 1862 to Eugenius Birch's design and built by Glasgow engineering firm Richard Laidlaw and Son. The pier cost £11,740 to build and originally comprised a promenade 468 yards long and 9 yards wide, extending to 18 yards wide at the pier-head. A historical Sooty glove puppet is on display, commemorating Harry Corbett's purchase of the original puppet there. The 1960s-built arcade sees about eleven million coins pass through its machines each year.

Nearby pubs: Shenanigans, 98 Promenade; Yates, 13-15 Market Street; The Mitre, West Street

Nearby cafes: Promenade, North Shore; Yoochat, 22 Bank Hey Street; Starbucks, Victoria Street

Nearby car parks: Promenade, North Shore; West Street Multistory, West Street; Filey Place Car Park, Filey Place

Nearest bus stop: Bank Hey Street, Foxhall

Nearest station: Blackpool North, Talbot Road

Nearby places to visit: Blackpool Tower; Blackpool Illuminations; Golden Mile; Central Pier, Blackpool; Grand Metropole Hotel

❏ **Date visited:**
Notes on visit:

Blackpool: South Pier

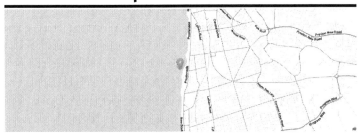

Promenade, FY4 1BB • blackpoolpiers.co.uk

South Pier, formerly known as Victoria Pier, is situated on the South Promenade and boasts several amusement and adrenaline rides. It opens annually from March to November. Construction of the pier began in 1892 by the Blackpool South Shore Pier & Pavilion Co. Ltd. It cost £50,000 to complete. It opened on Good Friday in 1893. The Grand Pavilion, which could accommodate up to 3,000 people, opened on May 20th of the same year. At 163 yards long, South Pier was the shortest of the three piers but had 36 shops, a bandstand, an ice-cream vendor, and a photograph stall. Initially, Victoria Pier was considered more 'upmarket' than North and Central piers and provided little entertainment. However, holidaymakers began visiting the South Shore in 1896 when a carousel was installed on the sand dunes. In 1930, the pier was renamed South Pier, and in 1938 the entrance was widened, with the Regal Pavilion constructed; this was damaged by fire in 1958 and then destroyed by another fire in 1964. It was replaced with a theatre, and in 1963, the Regal Theatre was converted into the Beachcomber Amusement Arcade.

Nearby pubs: The Velvet Coaster, 501-507 Promenade; The Gallant Pioneer, 11 Station Road; The Dutton Arms, 441 Promenade

Nearby cafes: Seagulls Nest, 3 Dean Street; Costa, Balmoral Road; Woodheads Cafe, 4 Simpson Street

Nearby car parks: Promenade, South Shore; Viking Hotel, Dean Street; Osborne Road Car Park, Osborne Road

Nearest bus stop: Promenade, South Shore

Nearest station: Blackpool Pleasure Beach, Ventnor Road

Nearby places to visit: Sandcastle Waterpark; Hot Ice Show; Blackpool Pleasure Beach

❏ **Date visited:**
Notes on visit:

Bognor Regis Pier

The Esplanade, PO21 1NE

Bognor Regis Pier is Grade II listed and was designed by Sir Charles Fox and J. W. Wilson; it opened on May 5, 1865, with a length of 1000 ft (305m). Over time, the pier underwent several developments, including the addition of a bandstand in 1880 and a seaward end pavilion in 1900. A small landing stage was also added in 1903, allowing paddle steamers to dock. During World War II, the pier was used as a Royal Navy observation station named HMS St Barbara. Unfortunately, the pier suffered storm damage in 1964 and 1965, causing the pavilion to sink into the sea. In December 1974, after two fires in three months, the pier was closed. An application was made in 1994 to demolish the remaining seaward end of the structure. The pier's legacy lives on through the International Bognor Birdman competition, an annual event for human-powered 'flying' machines. Contestants launch themselves from the end of the pier, with a prize awarded to the one who glides the furthest distance. The event started in nearby Selsey in 1971 and moved to Bognor in 1978.

Nearby pubs: Sheiks Nightclub, The Esplanade; Legends Sports Bar, The Esplanade; The Waterloo Inn, 14 Waterloo Square

Nearby cafes: Pier Coffee Shop, The Esplanade; The Dolphin Cafe, 5 Waterloo Square; Poppins Cafe, 64 High Street

Nearby car parks: Lennox Street, Bognor Regis; Chapel Street, Bognor Regis; Chapel Street, Bognor Regis

Nearest bus stop: Carlton Hotel, The Esplanade

Nearest station: Bognor Regis, Longford Road

Nearby places to visit: Butlins Bognor Regis

❏ **Date visited:**
Notes on visit:

Bournemouth: Boscombe Pier

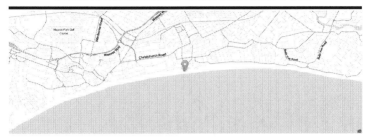

Promenade, BH5 1BN

A pier in Boscombe was proposed in 1884 as a visitor attraction. The resulting pier, 200 yards long and 11 yards wide, featured a wrought iron girder frame supporting timber decking, with a 40-yard-long pier head and a landing stage on each side. Designed by architect James Stuart Campbell McEwan-Brown, Boscombe Pier was opened with great fanfare on 29 July 1889 by the Duke of Argyll. The pier head was added in 1926, and the structure was partially demolished during World War II as a countermeasure against invasion. Remaining derelict for several years, the pier was fully reopened in 1962. The Grade II listed entrance building, designed by borough architect John Burton, was restored in 2007 along with the pier neck, with new decking, lighting, windbreak screen, and a viewing and fishing platform end section replacing the derelict Mermaid Amusement Hall. In 2014, an interactive musical walkway was added, featuring 88 custom-made chimes that play 'I Do Like To be Beside the Seaside' when struck in the correct order.

Nearby pubs: Chaplins, 529 533 Christchurch Road; Conroy's Bar, 33 Sea Road; Obsidian, 14 Sea Road

Nearby cafes: The Prom Diner, Undercliff Drive; Santa Cruz, 511 Christchurch Road; Rosie's, Roumelia Lane

Nearby car parks: Overstrand, The Marina; Boscombe Spa Road, Springbourne; Roumelia Lane, Springbourne

Nearest bus stop: Boscombe Pier, Sea Road

Nearest station: Pokesdown, Hannington Place

Nearby places to visit: O2 Academy Bournemouth; Boscombe Surf Reef

❏ **Date visited:**
Notes on visit:

Bournemouth Pier

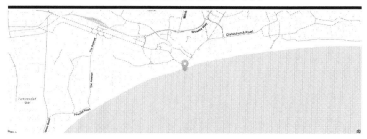

Pier Approach, BH2 5AA

The first pier in Bournemouth was a short wooden jetty completed in 1856, later replaced by a longer wooden pier which opened on 17 September 1861; worm attacks led to the wooden piles being replaced with cast iron in 1866. Later storm damage led to the original pier being demolished; over the next three years, a new pier designed by Eugenius Birch was built, costing £2,600 and opening on 11 August 1880. The open promenade measured 838 ft long and featured a bandstand added in 1885. Covered shelters were also added, and two extensions in 1894 and 1909 increased the pier's length to over 1000 ft. Bournemouth Pier was substantially demolished on 5 July 1940 as a precaution against German invasion, similar to other piers in the south and east. Repairs were completed in August 1946, and the pier head was refurbished in 1950. A decade later, the substructure was rebuilt in concrete to support a new pier theatre. In 1979 the old shoreward end buildings were replaced with a two-story octagonal leisure complex, and the pier neck was reconstructed in concrete, giving it a bridge-like appearance.

Nearby pubs: Hot Rocks, Pier Approach; Urban Jungle, Exeter Park Road; The Brasshaus, 8-9 Westover Road

Nearby cafes: Coffee Reef, Pier Approach; The Prom, Pier Approach; The Terrace, Westover Road

Nearby car parks: East Cliff Slope, Lansdowne; Bath Road North, Westover Road; Bath Road South, Bath Road

Nearest bus stop: Royal Bath Hotel, Bath Road

Nearest station: Bournemouth, Upside Station Approach

Nearby places to visit: Bournemouth International Centre; Russell-Cotes Art Gallery & Museum; Pavilion Theatre; West Cliff Railway; East Cliff Railway; Winter Gardens

❏ **Date visited:**
Notes on visit:

Brighton Palace Pier

Madeira Drive, BN2 1ET • www.brightonpier.co.uk

The Brighton Palace Pier, also known as Brighton Pier or the Palace Pier, is a popular Grade II* listed pleasure pier. It was established in 1899, making it the third pier to be constructed in Brighton after the Royal Suspension Chain Pier and the West Pier. Today, it is the only pier still in operation. It is 1,722 feet long, containing 85 miles of planking; it is illuminated by 67,000 lightbulbs. Originally intended as a replacement for the Chain Pier, which collapsed in 1896, the Palace Pier quickly became popular and was a frequently visited theatre and entertainment venue by 1911. Both Stan Laurel and Charlie Chaplin performed at the pier, which has been featured in many works of British culture, including Brighton Rock and Quadrophenia. In the 1920s, the pier was widened, and a distinctive clock tower was added. The theatre was demolished in 1986, changing the pier's character from seaside entertainment to an amusement park, with various fairground rides and roller coasters.

Nearby pubs: Glitter Ball, Madeira Drive; Horatio's Bar, Madeira Drive; Victoria's, Grand Junction Road

Nearby cafes: Moo Moo's Favourites, Grand Junction Road; Coffee Trader, Madeira Drive; Grand Junction Road, Brunswick

Nearby car parks: Charles Street, Queen's Park; Avenue, The Lanes; Van Alen Mews, Kemptown

Nearest bus stop: Palace Pier, Grand Junction Road

Nearest station: Aquarium, Madeira Drive

Nearby places to visit: Royal Pavilion; Volk's Electric Railway; Brighton Museum & Art Gallery; Holy Trinity Church, Brighton; Brighton Fishing Museum; Brighton Wheel

❏ **Date visited:**
Notes on visit:

Burnham Pier

Esplanade, TA8 1BG

Built in 1914, Burnham Pier measures 37 metres (121 ft) in length. It was built of reinforced concrete, which was a departure from the steel and cast iron used in previous pier constructions. The pier is occupied by a building known as the pavilion, which houses a 100-seat café, a bingo hall and an amusements arcade. At low tide, the pier can be up to 1.5 miles (2.4 km) from the sea due to the high tidal range of the Bristol Channel. It was refurbished for its centenary in 2014, including a new seating area with a retractable roof, and again in 2020. On 5 August 2021, Burnham Pier suffered from a severe fire that began in a wood and refuse storage area at the seaward end of the pavilion. The pier reopened for business a few days later, though part of the structure was initially cordoned off for safety reasons. The Burnham Pier remains a beloved landmark in the area, awaiting full restoration.

Nearby pubs: Chaplin's, Adam Street; The Railway, College Street; The Reed's Arms, Pier Street

Nearby cafes: Bay View Café, South Esplanade; Oxford Street, Burnham-on-Sea and Highbridge; Starbucks, Hall Terrace

Nearby car parks: College Street, Burnham-on-Sea and Highbridge; Myrtle Drive, Burnham-on-Sea and Highbridge; Princess Street, Burnham-on-Sea and Highbridge

Nearest bus stop: Old Pier Tavern, Pier Street

Nearest station: Highbridge and Burnham, Market Street

Nearby places to visit: Apex Leisure and Wildlife Park

❏ **Date visited:**
Notes on visit:

18

Clacton-on-Sea: Clacton Pier

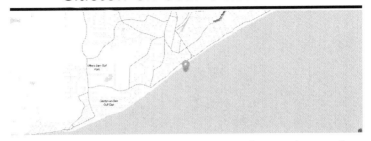

Kings Promenade, CO15 1FT • www.clactonpier.co.uk

Clacton Pier has a long and interesting history, having been officially opened on July 27, 1871, and serving as the first building in the then-new resort town. Initially, the pier was a wooden structure that was 160 yards long and 4 yards wide, and served as a landing point for goods and passengers. Over the years, the pier has undergone many changes and improvements to become the award-winning attraction it is today. In 1893, the pier was lengthened to 1180 ft and entertainment facilities, including a pavilion and a waiting room, were added to accommodate the growing number of visitors. In the post-World War I era, the pier was bought by Ernest Kingsman, and his family owned it until 1971. Kingsman added a theatre, dance hall, casino, open-air stage, swimming pool, and a roller coaster. In 1994, the pier was purchased by the Harrison family, who undertook a major modernization project to attract 21st-century day trippers.

Nearby pubs: The Boardwalk, Pier Gap; Playas @ The Pavilion, Marine Parade East; Silver Sand Lounge, Orwell Road

Nearby cafes: The Lagoon Tea Room, Pier Gap; The Terrace, Kings Promenade; JD's Pie & Mash, 17 Pallister Road

Nearby car parks: Colne Road, Clacton-on-Sea; Agate Rd, Agate Road; Orwell Road, Clacton-on-Sea

Nearest bus stop: Marine Parade East, Clacton-on-Sea

Nearest station: Clacton-on-Sea, Railway Terrace

Nearby places to visit: West Cliff Theatre, Clacton Cliffs

❏ **Date visited:**
Notes on visit:

Cleethorpes Pier

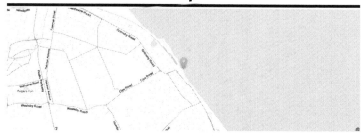

Central Promenade, DN35 8SF

Cleethorpes Pier was opened on August Bank Holiday in 1873 and was built by Head Wrightson at a cost of £8,000, which was financed by the Manchester, Sheffield and Lincolnshire Railway. At its original length of 1,200 feet, it was designed to span the unusually large distance between low and high tide limits. The pier comprised a timber deck and pavilion supported on iron piles, with a section being cut out of the pier during the Second World War to impede its use in any German invasion attempt. The pier has undergone several changes in ownership and usage over the years. The original pavilion was destroyed by fire in 1903, but a new one was built in 1905, halfway along the pier, which offered a venue for dances and concerts. In 1968, a £50,000 investment modernized the 600-seat concert hall, cafe and bar. After a stint as an amusement park and then a nightclub, the pier was refurbished in 2015, reopening as a venue for fine dining, traditional pub food and afternoon tea. In 2016, the pier was purchased by Papa's Fish and Chip chain and became the largest fish and chip restaurant in the country.

Nearby pubs: Figs, Mill Place; Number 2 Refreshment Room, Station Approach; The Foundry Bar & Kitchen, Station Road

Nearby cafes: Hawaiian Eye Cafe (Closed), Central Promenade; Cafe Rock, Central Promenade; Browns Cafe, North Promenade

Nearby car parks: Central Promenade Car Park, Humber Street; Alexandra Road, Cleethorpes; Yarra Road Car Park, Yarra Road

Nearest bus stop: Sea Road, Cleethorpes

Nearest station: Cleethorpes, North Promenade

Nearby places to visit: Cleethorpes Coast Light Railway, Pleasure Island Theme Park

❏ **Date visited:**
Notes on visit:

Clevedon Pier

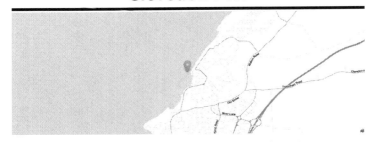

Marine Parade, BS21 7QS • www.clevedonpier.com

Clevedon Pier is a picturesque seaside pier in Somerset, on the east shore of the Severn Estuary. Sir John Betjeman described it as "the most beautiful pier in England", and it was designated a Grade I listed building in 2001. The pier was constructed during the 1860s to draw tourists and establish a ferry port for rail passengers to South Wales. Stretching 312 metres (1,024 feet) in length, the pier comprises eight spans supported by steel rails, topped by wooden decking and a pavilion at the pier head. The pier opened in 1869, and for nearly a century it functioned as an embarkation point for paddle steamer excursions. In 1970, two of the spans collapsed during stress testing, prompting demolition proposals. However, local fundraising and heritage grants allowed for the pier to be dismantled, restored and reassembled; it reopened in 1989. Today, the pier serves as a landing stage for steamers and is a popular attraction for tourists and anglers.

Nearby pubs: Moon and Sixpence, 15 The Beach; The Royal Oak, 35 Copse Road; The Little Harp Inn, Elton Road

Nearby cafes: Pagoda Tea Room, Marine Parade; Hut Café, Alexandra Road; Scarletts, 20 The Beach

Nearby car parks: Beach Mews, Walton Park; Elton Road, West End; Burden Park, West End

Nearest bus stop: Elton Road, West End

Nearest station: Yatton, Station Approach

Nearby places to visit: Curzon Community Cinema, Clevedon

❏ **Date visited:**
Notes on visit:

Cromer Pier

Esplanade, NR27 9HF • www.cromer-pier.com

Cromer Pier is a well-known Grade II listed seaside pier on the north coast of Norfolk. The pier is home to the Cromer Lifeboat Station and the Pavilion Theatre. The pier has a rich history and has seen many changes since its inception in 1391, when it was in the form of a jetty. The pier has been destroyed and rebuilt over the years, with the most recent reconstruction work completed in 2013. The pier's history is claimed to go back to Queen Elizabeth I's time: in 1582, she granted rights to the inhabitants of Cromer to export wheat, barley and malt here. In 1822, a 210-foot (64 m) long jetty was built of cast iron, but it was destroyed by a storm 24 years later. A wooden structure was then built, which lasted until 1897 when it was damaged beyond repair. In 1902, a new pier was completed and opened to the public.

Nearby pubs: The Albion, Surrey Street; The White Horse, West Street; The Fishing Boat, High Street

Nearby cafes: About with Friends, 9 Tucker Street; Grey Seal Coffee Roasters, 24 High Street; North Sea Coffee Co, Esplanade

Nearby car parks: Co-op, Corner Street; Surrey Street, Cromer; Esplanade, Cromer

Nearest bus stop: Church Street, adj

Nearest station: Cromer, Holt Road

Nearby places to visit: Cromer Museum; Old Town Hall Theatre

❏ **Date visited:**
Notes on visit:

Deal Pier

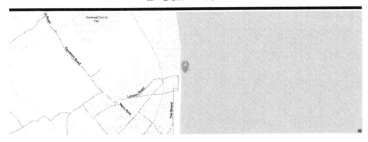

A258, CT14 6HZ

Deal Pier is the last remaining fully intact leisure pier in the county and has a rich history dating back to the 19th century. The first pier was built in 1838 by Sir John Rennie and was destroyed during a storm in 1857. The second pier, designed by Eugenius Birch, opened in 1864 and sustained impact damage several times during the 1870s. It was acquired by Deal Council in 1920 and survived until the Second World War when it was severely damaged by a mined Dutch ship. Permission to demolish the pier was authorised by Winston Churchill, leaving just the shore-side toll house, itself later demolished in 1954. The current pier opened to the public in 1957. It was designed by Sir W. Halcrow & Partners and is made predominantly of concrete-clad steel. The pier has undergone extensive refurbishment and repair over the years, with major work taking place in 1997 and 2018. Today the pier is a popular sport fishing venue, featuring a cafe, bar, lounge and fishing decks.

Nearby pubs: The Bohemian, 47 Beach Street; The Port Arms, 10 Beach Street; The King's Head, 9 Beach Street

Nearby cafes: ARouteOne On The Prom, 70 Beach Street; Wellington Cafe, 27 Beach Street; The Lane, 15 South Court

Nearby car parks: Beach Street Car Park, Market Street; Middle Street Car Park, Middle Street; Beach Street On Street Parking, Coppin Street

Nearest bus stop: Pier, Five Step Alley

Nearest station: Deal, London Road

Nearby places to visit: Deal Castle 🏛; Deal Timeball; Kent Museum of the Moving Image

---

❏ **Date visited:**
Notes on visit:

Eastbourne Pier

Grand Parade, BN21 3EH

Eastbourne Pier was first proposed in 1863 as a 1000-foot long structure, but it was eventually built on the present site at the junction of Grand and Marine Parades, creating the easterly end of a shingle bay. The pier was opened in 1870 but it was not completed until two years later. It is roughly 300 metres (1000 ft) long and is built on stilts that rest in cups on the sea-bed, allowing the whole structure to move during rough weather. A domed 400-seater pavilion was constructed at the seaward end in 1888, and a 1000-seater theatre, bar, camera obscura and office suite replaced this in 1899/1901. Paddle steamers ran trips from the pier along the south coast and across the Channel to Boulogne from 1906 until the outbreak of the Second World War. During the war, part of the decking was removed, and machine guns were installed. In 2014, the pier suffered a fire that ripped through a large amount of the central domed building, though it has since been fully repaired and reopened. Today, the pier is home to various attractions, including amusements, a nightclub and food outlets. The tower at the end of the pier is often used as a viewing point during the annual air show.

Nearby pubs: 1901 Grand Parade, Roselands; Ocean View, Marine Parade; The Shore Bar & Grill, Cavendish Place

Nearby cafes: Victorian Tea Room, Grand Parade; The Pier Hotel Coffee Lounge, Cavendish Place; Costa, 133-135 Seaside Road

Nearby car parks: Burlington Hotel Private Car Park, Elms Road; Hartington Place, Roselands; Trinity Place, Roselands

Nearest bus stop: Eastbourne Pier, Grand Parade

Nearest station: Eastbourne, Ashford Road

Nearby places to visit: Eastbourne Redoubt; Towner Gallery

❏ **Date visited:**
Notes on visit:

Falmouth: Prince of Wales Pier

Prince of Wales Pier, TR11 3DF

Prince of Wales Pier had its foundation stone laid in 1903 by the then Prince of Wales, later George V, and was named after him; it officially opened in 1905. Designed by engineer W H Tressider, the pier features a combination of solid groin and open construction with reinforced concrete piles. During World War II, the pier was taken over by American forces and only reopened to the public in April 1951. Since then, there have been two main post-war restorations, in 1951 and 1987. The pier has a memorial dedicated to the St Nazaire raid, during which five Victory Crosses were awarded, and a service of remembrance takes place at the pier every March. It was also used as an embarkation point for the D-Day landings.

Nearby pubs: Prince of Wales, 4 Market Street; Finn M'Coul's, Market Street; Beerwolf Books, 3-4 Market Street

Nearby cafes: The Pier Cafe, Prince of Wales Pier; Caffè Nero, 10 Market Street; Cavindish Coffee House, Market Street

Nearby car parks: Vernon Place, Falmouth; Church Street Car Park, Church Street; Well Lane Short Stay Car Park, Well Lane

Nearest bus stop: Prince of Wales Pier, Falmouth

Nearest station: Falmouth Town, Avenue Road

Nearby places to visit: National Maritime Museum Cornwall; Falmouth Art Gallery

❑ **Date visited:**
Notes on visit:

Felixstowe Pier

The Promenade, IP11 2AB

Felixstowe Pier was opened to the public in August 1905 and its length of 2,640 feet (800 m) made it one of the longest piers in the country. The pier was constructed using timber instead of iron, which was uncommon for the period. It had its own railway station and offered steamer services to various destinations. However, during the war, the pier was sectioned to reduce the risk of enemy invasion, and after the war, it never fully recovered. Eventually, the pierhead was demolished because it had been left to deteriorate. Over the years, various renovation plans were proposed. Finally, in August 2017, a new shore-end structure was opened to the public at a cost of £3m as part of a wider regeneration scheme for the local area. The new structure includes a bowling alley, arcade machines and wraparound boardwork. Although visitors are not able to walk the entire length of the pier due to safety concerns, the original decking extending over the sea still remains.

Nearby pubs: The Boardwalk Cafe Bar, Undercliff Road West; The Skye Lounge, 55-57 Undercliff Road West; Felsto Arms, 8 Sea Road

Nearby cafes: Beach House, Undercliff Road West; The Pantry, 65 Undercliff Road West; Gulliver's Wife, 47 Undercliff Road West

Nearby car parks: The Promenade, Old Felixstowe; Convalescent Hill, The Promenade; Granville Road, Grange Farm

Nearest bus stop: Car Park, Convalescent Path

Nearest station: Felixstowe, High Road West

Nearby places to visit: Felixstowe Museum

❏ **Date visited:**

Notes on visit:

Folkestone Harbour Arm

Harbour Arm, CT20 1QH • www.folkestoneharbour.com

Folkestone Harbour has a rich history dating back to the 16th century. In the 19th century, the Earl of Radnor petitioned for the construction of a stone harbour and pier, which was built by Thomas Telford in 1809. By the end of the century, the pier was extended by 900 feet to form a sheltering arm with berths for steamers. During World War I, Folkestone Harbour became a huge embarkation point for British troops heading to France and the Western Front, handling 10,463,834 military mailbags and 120,000 war refugees. In World War II, the port closed to civilian boat usage and 44,000 personnel used the port during the Dunkirk Evacuation. In 2001, all ferry services stopped, and by 2010, only ten boats with thirty men were employed in the fishing industry. A plan was commissioned for the development of the harbour and seafront in 2010, and stonework and original steelwork on the harbour arm were carefully restored. The area was opened up to the public as a new pier and promenade in the summer of 2015.

Nearby pubs: The Mariner, The Stade; The Pilot, Harbour Arm; The Ship Inn, The Stade

Nearby cafes: Harbour Coffee Co, Harbour Arm; Captains Table, 26 The Stade; Harbour Approach Road, Foord

Nearby car parks: Harbour Arm, East Cliff; The Stade, Foord; Harbour Approach Road, Foord

Nearest bus stop: Radnor Bridge, Radnor Bridge Road

Nearest station: Folkestone Central, Kingsnorth Gardens

Nearby places to visit: Leas Lift, Lower Leas Coastal Park, Folkestone Roman Villa

❏ **Date visited:**
Notes on visit:

Gravesend Town Pier

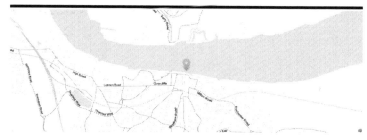

Town Pier, DA11 0BJ

Designed by William Tierney Clark, the pier was constructed in 1834 on the site of the earlier Town Quay. The pier served over three million passengers between 1835 and 1842, making it a bustling hub of activity. However, with the arrival of the railways around 1900, the pier fell into disuse and was abandoned for several decades. In 2000, the Gravesham Borough Council stepped in and restored the site with the help of several organizations, including English Heritage and the Heritage Lottery Fund. The renovation project was completed in 2002 and included the addition of a restaurant and a bar to the pier. The restored Gravesend Town Pier opened to the public and was initially successful, but it later became a financial failure. Despite this setback, the Gravesend Town Pier remains an important historical site and is the oldest surviving cast iron pier in the world. It is also a Grade II* listed building. Since 2012, the pier has been home to the Gravesend-Tilbury Ferry, which provides transportation for commuters and tourists alike. In November 2022, Thames Clippers announced that they had purchased the pier with the aim of operating a long-term River Bus service from Gravesend.

Nearby pubs: Three Daws, 7 Town Pier; LV21 Crooked Lane, Milton; Rum Puncheon, 87 West Street

Nearby cafes: Mug and Meeple Gamer Cafe, Town Pier Square; Sizzling Cafe, 62 High Street; Maries Tea Room, 23 High Street

Nearby car parks: West Street, Church Street; Regents Court, Milton; West Street, Milton

Nearest bus stop: West Street, Crooked Lane

Nearest station: Gravesend, Clive Road

Nearby places to visit: Tilbury Fort ▦; New Tavern Fort; Milton Chantry ▦

❏ **Date visited:**
Notes on visit:

Gravesend: Royal Terrace Pier

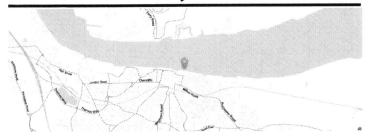

Royal Pier Road, DA12 2AZ

Royal Terrace Pier, located in Gravesend, is owned and managed by the Port of London Authority (PLA) and is situated next to the PLA's headquarters at London River House. This Grade II listed pier was constructed in 1844 by the Gravesend Freehold Investment Company at an expense of £9,200. It was designed by John Baldry Redman, an architect known for his work in the Gothic Revival style. In 1865, Princess Alexandra arrived at the pier to marry the Prince of Wales, who later became King Edward VII. The pier was also home to the Gravesend Lifeboat Station, which moved to the pontoon at the pier's end in June 2007. The Royal Terrace Pier Estate Company Limited was established in 1893 to manage the pier, but it was dissolved in 2012.

Nearby pubs: TJ's, 15 Milton Road; George Inn, 38 Queen Street; LV21 Crooked Lane, Milton

Nearby cafes: Promenade Cafe, Gordon Promenade; Coffee Table Shop, 6 Queen Street; Mug and Meeple Gamer Cafe, Town Pier Square

Nearby car parks: The Terrace, Milton; Royal Pier Road, Milton; Commercial Place, Milton

Nearest bus stop: Clock Tower Harmer Street, Harmer Street

Nearest station: Gravesend, Clive Road

Nearby places to visit: Tilbury Fort 🏰; New Tavern Fort; Milton Chantry 🏰

❏ **Date visited:**
Notes on visit:

Great Yarmouth: Britannia Pier

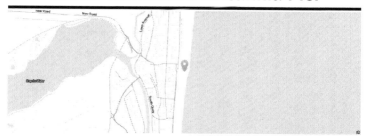

Marine Parade, NR30 2DL • www.britannia-pier.co.uk

Britannia Pier dates back to 1858, when it was first constructed by Alfred William Morant. The original pier was 700 feet long, but it was reduced in length due to storm damage. Unfortunately, it was eventually demolished in 1899. However, a new pier was built in its place in 1901, designed by engineers Joseph and Arthur Mayoh. The new pier had a Grand Pavilion, which burned down in 1909. A second Pavilion was built, which was destroyed in 1914 by militant suffragettes. A third Pavilion was quickly constructed and opened in 1914. The pier has had its fair share of further damage and destruction throughout its history. The Floral Hall Ballroom was destroyed by fire in 1932, and the Grand Ballroom was destroyed in 1954 along with the third Pavilion. Despite these setbacks, the pier has remained a popular attraction for visitors to Great Yarmouth. Today, the pier is owned by Triangle Amusements and continues to provide live theatre shows, food outlets, bars, amusements and fairground rides.

Nearby pubs: Long Johns, Marine Parade; Pier Tavern, Marine Parade; Pub on the Prom, 76-77 Marine Parade

Nearby cafes: Sands Cafe, Marine Parade; Shemara Beach Refreshments, Marine Parade; Princes Tea Rooms, Marine Parade

Nearby car parks: Euston Road Car Park, North Drive; Marine Parade, Northgate; Anchor Gardens Car Park, Marine Parade

Nearest bus stop: Britannia Pier, adj

Nearest station: Great Yarmouth, Lime Kiln Walk

Nearby places to visit: Wellington Pier; Great Yarmouth Row Houses ▣; Time and Tide Museum; Lydia Eva (steam drifter); Norfolk Nelson Museum; Joyland (Great Yarmouth); The Tolhouse

---

❏ **Date visited:**

Notes on visit:

Great Yarmouth: Wellington Pier

Shadingfield Close, NR30 3JG • www.wellington-pier.co.uk

Wellington Pier is a historic wooden pier. It was opened in 1853 and was designed by P Ashcroft. It cost £6,776 to build and was 700 feet long. In its first year of operation, it made an impressive profit of £581. However, the pier faced competition when a second pier was built nearby five years later. By 1899, the pier was struggling and was bailed out by the Great Yarmouth Corporation for £1,250. They had plans to improve the entertainment and amusement of the pier and opened a new Pavilion in 1903. The pier was leased by entertainer Jim Davidson in 1996, who invested £750,000 to refurbish the inside of the pier. The theatre on the pier was partially demolished in 2005, but the front part of the pier was redeveloped as an amusement arcade. The pier's old theatre was converted into a large bowling alley and bar in 2008, with restored steel and ironwork visible in the new building. The restoration of an 80-foot-long stained-glass picture found during the removal of the original Wellington pier theatre structure is expected to form the centrepiece of a new entrance.

Nearby pubs: Marine, 15 Marine Parade; Barking Smack, 16 Marine Parade; Duke of Wellington, 37 Saint Peter's Road

Nearby cafes: Beach House Cafe, Marine Parade; HJ's Diner, Marine Parade; Costa, Marine Parade

Nearby car parks: Marine Parade, Barrack Estate; Shadingfield Close, Barrack Estate; Kimberley Terrace, Barrack Estate

Nearest bus stop: Wellington Pier, adj

Nearest station: Great Yarmouth, Lime Kiln Walk

Nearby places to visit: Great Yarmouth Row Houses ■; Time and Tide Museum; Great Yarmouth Pleasure Beach; Lydia Eva (steam drifter); Norfolk Nelson Museum

❑ **Date visited:**
Notes on visit:

Harwich: Ha'penny Pier

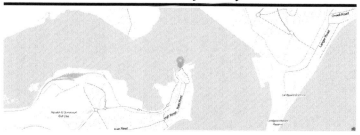

The Quay, CO12 3HH

Construction on Harwich pier commenced in 1852, and it was inaugurated in 1853, earning its name from the ½d toll charged at the time. It is one of the country's few surviving wooden piers. Initially double its current length, the pier lost half its structure to a fire in 1927. Historically, it was a favoured departure point for paddle steamers until after World War I. The Pier Ticket Office, a quintessential late 19th-century architectural gem, now houses the Ha'penny Pier Visitor Centre, managed by the Harwich Society and highlighting early voyages of exploration. The area enclosed by the pier is known as the Pound and harbours the remnants of the once-impressive 19th-century fishing fleet. The pier also features a café, a seafood kiosk, and shower facilities for visiting yacht crews. Additionally, the pier accommodates the lifeboat house for the RNLI inshore rescue boat. Today, the Victorian pier attracts crabbers, day-trippers and fishermen.

Nearby pubs: The Alma, 25 Kings Head Street; The Globe, Kings Quay Street; The British Flag, West Street

Nearby cafes: The Cafe on the Pier, The Quay; Café on the Green, Harbour Crescent; Cafe In The Park, High Street

Nearby car parks: The Quay, Harwich; The Angel, Harwich; Eastgate Street, Harwich

Nearest bus stop: Quay, West Street

Nearest station: Harwich Town, Station Road

Nearby places to visit: Harwich Redoubt

❏ **Date visited:**
Notes on visit:

32

Hastings Pier

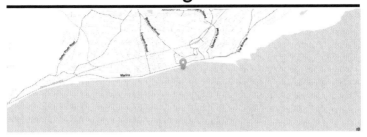

White Rock, TN34 1JU

Hastings Pier was opened on 5 August 1872 by the then Lord Warden of the Cinque Ports, the Earl of Granville, and designed by Eugenius Birch. The pier enjoyed its prime in the 1930s, with the extension buildings receiving an art deco facelift and a theatre rebuild. More renovation followed its temporary closure during WWII, and in 1966 it housed the Hastings Embroidery during the 900th anniversary celebrations of the Battle of Hastings. The original 2,000 seater pavilion was destroyed by fire in 1917, but was eventually replaced in 1922. However, the structure suffered major storm damage in 1990, requiring a £1 million refurbishment. In 1996, it was put up for sale, but potential buyers were reluctant and it was closed in 1999. The pier eventually reopened under new ownership in 2002 but faced further challenges in 2006 when part of its structure was deemed unsafe and closed to the general public. The pier suffered considerable damage from a storm in 2008, and extensive fire damage in 2010, with 95% of the superstructure destroyed. Following a renovation project, the pier reopened to the public in 2016.

Nearby pubs: Brewing Brothers Courtyard, White Rock; French's, 24-25 Robertson Street; TinTins, 21 Robertson Street

Nearby cafes: White Rock, America Ground; Bullet Coffee House, 38-38a; Stooges Coffee House, 4 Trinity Street

Nearby car parks: Pier Underground Car Park, White Rock; Falaise Hall Car Park, Falaise Road; St. Margaret's Road, America Ground

Nearest bus stop: White Rock Gardens, Cambridge Road

Nearest station: Hastings, Station Approach

Nearby places to visit: St. Clements Caves; Hastings Museum and Art Gallery; West Hill Cliff Railway; Hastings Miniature Railway; Hastings Contemporary

❏ **Date visited:**
Notes on visit:

Herne Bay Pier

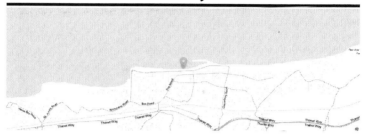

Central Parade, CT6 8SS • www.hernebaypier.org

Herne Bay Pier, the third pier to be built at the town, was notable for its 3,787 feet (1,154 m) length – the second longest in England when completed in 1899 – and for featuring in the opening sequence of Ken Russell's first feature film, French Dressing (1964). However, it was destroyed in a storm in 1978 and dismantled in 1980, leaving a stub with a sports centre at the landward end and part of the landing stage isolated at sea. Before the construction of Herne Bay Pier, there were two previous piers: an 1832 wooden deep-sea pier designed by Thomas Rhodes, assistant to Thomas Telford, and a second shorter iron version by Wilkinson & Smith, completed in 1873. The third pier was used by paddle steamers until 1963. The new 1899 restaurant at the pierhead later became a ticket office and cafe and still stands today: wooden, octagonal and domed. The 1910 Grand Pavilion survived in 1928 when the theatre, shops and Mazzoleni's cafe at the entrance were destroyed by fire. Efforts to redevelop Herne Bay pier have been ongoing for years, with various proposals and funding sources considered, but the pier remains in a crumbling state and its future is uncertain.

Nearby pubs: The Firkin Frog, Station Road; Four Fathoms, 2 High Street; The Pub, 73 Avenue Road

Nearby cafes: iFun Cafe, St George's Terrace; B2205 Oxenden, Canterbury; Makcari's The Bandstand, Central Parade

Nearby car parks: St George's Terrace, Oxenden; King's Road, Oxenden; Fleetwood Avenue, The Fairways

Nearest bus stop: Oxenden Street, Avenue Road

Nearest station: Herne Bay, The Circus

Nearby places to visit: Herne Bay Museum and Gallery

❑ **Date visited:**
Notes on visit:

34

Hythe Pier (Hants)

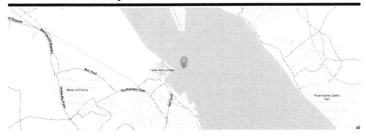

Shamrock Way, SO45 6DY

Hythe Pier, the Hythe Pier Railway and the Hythe Ferry form important transportation links between Southampton and the village of Hythe. The railway is the oldest continuously operating public pier train in the world. The ferry was due to stop operating at the end of 2022, but services continued in the hope that a new owner could be found. Hythe Pier stretches 700 yards (640 m) from the centre of Hythe to the deep water channel of Southampton Water, making it the 7th longest pier in the British Isles. It carries a pedestrian walkway and cycleway on its northern side and the Hythe Pier Railway on its southern side; during normal high tides, the pier is 4 feet (1.2 m) above the surface of the water. The pier was initially proposed in 1870, and a company formed to construct it obtained an Act of Parliament in 1871. However, this effort stalled, and a pier was not constructed. The pier eventually opened in 1881, having cost £7,000 to construct. The pier and its associated structures were awarded Grade II listed status in August 2021. The Hythe Pier Railway was constructed in 1922 on the southern side of the pier.

Nearby pubs: Seashells, The Promenade; The Lord Nelson, High Street; Shamrock Way, Hollybank

Nearby cafes: Costa, High Street; Black Wax Coffee and Records, High Street; Waterside Cafe, The Marsh

Nearby car parks: Shamrock Way, Hollybank; Knighton Centre Car Park, St John's Street; St John's Street Car Park, St John's Street

Nearest bus stop: Hythe Pier, Prospect Place

Nearest station: Hythe Pier, Shamrock Way

Nearby places to visit: Southampton Town Quay

❑ **Date visited:**
Notes on visit:

Lowestoft: Claremont Pier

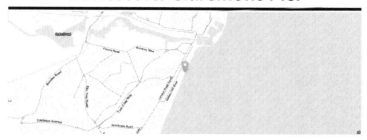

Claremont Road, NR33 0BS • www.claremontpier.co.uk

The Claremont Pier has a rich history dating back to 1903. Originally constructed as a mooring for Belle steamers, the pier was designed by D Fox and named after the nearby Claremont Road. It was extended in 1912 with the addition of a T-shaped landing head, bringing its length to 760 feet (230 m). During World War II, the pier was sectioned as a defense measure against the threat of invasion. After the war, a Bailey bridge was used to close the gap and the pier became an Army training centre until 1948. By the 1950s, the pier had fallen into disrepair, but it was repaired and reopened by actor George Studd. A storm in 1962 caused damage to the pier, reducing its length to 720 feet (220 m). After various changes of ownership, the pier reopened in July 2020 with a restaurant and ice cream kiosk. The pier also includes facilities such as an amusements arcade, bars and a new rooftop terrace. Future plans include reopening the pier deck and allowing people to walk along it.

Nearby pubs: The Plough & Sail, 212 London Road South; The Royal Oak, 195 London Road South; The Drifter, 218 London Road South

Nearby cafes: Desmond's Coffee Shop, 221b; Howards Tea Rooms, 177177a; Pinky's, Parade Road South

Nearby car parks: Claremont Road, Lowestoft; Kirkley Rise, Lowestoft; Marine Parade, Lowestoft

Nearest bus stop: Claremont Pier, Kirkley Cliff

Nearest station: Lowestoft, Denmark Road

Nearby places to visit: Mincarlo (trawler)

❏ **Date visited:**
Notes on visit:

Lowestoft: South Pier

A47, NR32 1BS

Originally engineered by William Cubitt, the pier opened in 1846 and was 1,320 feet (400 m) in length. The pier was built in association with harbour works and was described as having "one of the finest and most extensive promenades on the coast". In 1854, a reading room was added, and 30 years later, a jetty was constructed. However, both were destroyed during a fire in 1885 and were rebuilt around 1890. The pier was strengthened with concrete in 1928. During World War I, the pavilion on the pier was used as a headquarters for the Royal Naval Patrol Service's commanding officer. In the 1930s, the resort was at its height, and the pier was one of its main attractions. However, the replacement reading room and pavilion were heavily damaged during World War II and were subsequently demolished. A new pavilion was opened by the Duke of Edinburgh in 1956, and a shoreward leisure centre building was erected in 1975. The entire pier reopened in June 1993 following a £30,000 refurbishment by the council. Further refurbishments were undertaken in 2008. The pier was closed in 2013 due to public safety fears, but it was reopened in 2015 with the help of businessman Danny Steel and MP Peter Aldous.

Nearby pubs: Fishermans Wharf, Royal Plain; The Joseph Conrad Free House, 18-32 Station Square; Sir Toby's Beers, Royal Plain

Nearby cafes: Costa, 40 London Road North; Deans Beans, Royal Plain; The Pantry, 2 Surrey Street

Nearby car parks: A47 Lowestoft, East Suffolk; A47 Lowestoft, East Suffolk; Suffolk Road, Lowestoft

Nearest bus stop: Railway Station, Denmark Road

Nearest station: Lowestoft, Denmark Road

Nearby places to visit: Mincarlo (trawler); Claremont Pier

❑ **Date visited:**
Notes on visit:

Lytham St Anne's: St Anne's Pier

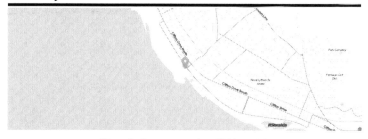

North Promenade, FY8 2NQ

St Anne's Pier is a Grade II listed Victorian era pier in the planned seaside resort of St Anne's-on-the-Sea. It was completed in 1885 by Alfred Dowson, making it one of the earliest public buildings in the town. Originally intended to be a place for sedate promenading, attractions were later added, including a Moorish-style pavilion in 1904 and the Floral Hall in 1910. The pier was reduced in length to 600 feet (180 m) after the demolition of the seaward end, following changes made to the estuary channels for improved access to Preston Dock that left the pier on dry land and ended its steamer services to Blackpool and Liverpool. In the 1950s, an amusement arcade was added, and by the 1970s, the pier's amusements included crazy golf, a miniature zoo and live theatre performances. The pier has suffered damage over the years, with the Moorish Pavilion destroyed by fire in 1974 and the Floral Hall destroyed in 1982. The seaward end of the pier was demolished, but the remaining 150 feet (46 m) were retained to protect the character of the pier. The pier's 21st-century attractions include an amusement arcade, cafés and shops.

Nearby pubs: Lord Derby, St Annes Road West; Pier Inn, 2 St Annes Road West; The Office, 18-20 Back St Anne's Road West

Nearby cafes: The Clock House, 67 Clifton Drive North; Water's Edge Cafe, South Promenade; Costa, Wood Street

Nearby car parks: North Promenade, St Annes; Clifton Drive North, St Annes; Fylde Council Public Offices Car Park, Clifton Drive South

Nearest bus stop: St David's Road North, St Annes

Nearest station: St Annes-on-the-Sea, Back Glen Eldon Road

Nearby places to visit: Lytham Windmill and Lifeboat Museum

❑ **Date visited:**
Notes on visit:

Paignton Pier

Eastern Esplanade, TQ3 2NJ • paigntonpier.co.uk

Paignton Pier is a historic pleasure pier that was financed by local barrister Arthur Hyde Dendy and designed by George Soudon Bridgman. The pier was built in 1878 and opened to the public in June 1879. It was 780 feet long, featuring a grand pavilion at the seaward end that hosted various forms of entertainment, including singing, dancing, recitals and music hall shows. In 1919, the pier-head and its associated buildings were destroyed in a fire, leading to a period of decline. During World War II, the pier was sectioned as a defence measure for fear of German invasion, but it was eventually repaired once hostilities had ceased. In 1980, a major redevelopment project was undertaken, including the widening of the shoreward end and the construction of stylish pavilions that remain today. The pier now comprises an entrance building at the shoreward end and several individual pavilion buildings connected along the neck, forming a single amusement arcade. At the pier-head, there is an open amusement area that contains karts, slides, and a carousel.

Nearby pubs: Inn on the Green, Esplanade Road; Harbour Light, North Quay; The Boathouse (closed), Promenade

Nearby cafes: The Harbour Tearoom And Bistro, Roundham Road; Bayside Cafe, Marine Drive; Amore, Torbay Road

Nearby car parks: Esplanade Road, Roundham; Eastern Esplanade, Roundham; Palace Hotel Parking, Esplanade Road

Nearest bus stop: Redcliffe Lodge, Esplanade Road

Nearest station: Paignton Queens Park, Great Western Road

Nearby places to visit: Kirkham House ▥; Splashdown Quaywest

❏ **Date visited:**
Notes on visit:

Ryde Pier

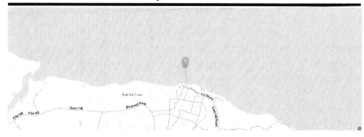

PO33 2HE

Ryde Pier, located on the Isle of Wight, is the world's oldest seaside pleasure pier. Built in the early 19th century, it was designed by John Kent of Southampton and opened on 26 July 1814. Before the pier was built, passengers had to come ashore on the back of a porter and then walk across wet sand before reaching the town. The original pier was wholly timber and measured 576 yards, but extensions brought the overall length to 745 yards by 1833. The pier has since undergone various modifications, including the addition of a second 'tramway' pier in 1864, a third pier in 1880, and a concert pavilion in 1895. Today, Ryde Pier is still a gateway for passenger traffic to and from the Isle of Wight, with Island Line trains running from Ryde Pier Head railway station at the pier head and the Wightlink catamaran running regularly between Ryde and Portsmouth. The pier is also open to vehicles and pedestrians, with panoramic views across the Solent to Portsmouth visible from the pier head. In 2014, the pier celebrated its 200th anniversary, and in 2020, a plan to reinstate the disused tramway pier as a pedestrian and cyclist route was announced as part of a wider regeneration project.

Nearby pubs: The King Lud, 2 Esplanade; Heron Lounge, 2A; Bar 74 74 Union Street, Pelhamfield

Nearby cafes: Seagull Cafe, Ryde Pier; 1 Esplanade, Pelhamfield; The Alamo, 56 Esplanade

Nearby car parks: Ryde Pier Carpark, Ryde Pier; Wightlink Staff Parking, Ryde Pier; Staff, Esplanade

Nearest bus stop: Ryde, Transport Interchange

Nearest station: Ryde Pier Head, Ryde Pier

Nearby places to visit: Isle of Wight Bus & Coach Museum

❏ **Date visited:**
Notes on visit:

Saltburn-by-the-Sea: Saltburn Pier

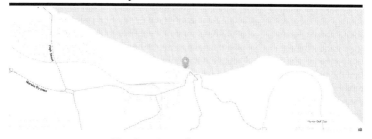

Marine Parade, TS12 1DP

Saltburn Pier is the last remaining pier in Yorkshire, and was built in 1867 by the Saltburn Pier Company, following the arrival of the Stockton and Darlington Railway in the area. The pier opened in May 1869, with a steamer landing stage at the head of the pier and two circular kiosks at the entrance. In the first six months of operation, there were 50,000 toll-paying visitors. Access to the pier was difficult from the town due to the steep cliff, so the Cliff Hoist was built which allowed 20 people to be lowered by rope to beach level. The pier was damaged by a gale in 1875, which removed 300 feet of the structure at the seaward end, leaving a redeveloped pier of 1,250 feet. The opening of the Cliff Lift in the 1880s allowed the pier company to undertake a development of facilities, including a saloon at the pier head, gas lighting along the entire length, and a bandstand. The pier was purchased by the council in 1938, and during World War II, part of the deck was removed by the Royal Engineers to guard against Nazi invasion. The pier has since suffered damage from storms, with piles being lost and the pier head being lost and the deck being damaged. The pier was refurbished and reopened in 1978/9.

Nearby pubs: The Alexandra Vaults, Marine Parade; The Guns Bar, 15 Milton Street; The Victoria, 3-5 Dundas Street East

Nearby cafes: Surf's Up, Saltburn Bank; The Vista Mar, Saltburn Road; Camfields Espresso Bar, Saltburn Road

Nearby car parks: Marine Parade, Old Saltburn; Marine Parade, Old Saltburn; Saltburn Road, Old Saltburn

Nearest bus stop: The Promenade, Saltburn Road

Nearest station: Pier, Marine Parade

Nearby places to visit: Saltburn Miniature Railway

❏ **Date visited:**

Notes on visit:

Sandown Pier

Esplanade, PO36 8JX

Sandown Pier's construction began in 1876, following the passing of a bill in Parliament in 1864. The first section of the pier was opened to the public in 1878 and measured 360 feet (110 m) in length. However, it wasn't until 1895 that the pier was extended to its full intended length of 870 feet (270 m), with a breadth of 24 feet (7.3 m) and a head area of 107 feet (33 m) by 93 feet (28 m). Over the years, Sandown Pier has undergone several renovations and improvements, including the construction of a pavilion in 1934, which cost £26,000, and the restoration of the pier following a devastating fire in 1989 that caused an estimated £2,000,000 in damages. Today, the pier offers a range of indoor amenities, including cafes, an amusement arcade, a bowling alley, and an indoor crazy golf course. At the seaward end of the pier, visitors can enjoy an outdoor funfair and landing stage.

Nearby pubs: Scruffy Jacks, Esplanade; Flanagans, 7 Pier Street; The Cellar Bar, 26B

Nearby cafes: The Icecream Parlour, Esplanade; Boardwalk Cafe, Esplanade; The Beach Cafe, 9 Pier Street

Nearby car parks: Esplanade, Sandown; Esplanade, Yaverland; Beachfield Road, Sandown

Nearest bus stop: Pier Street, Beachfield Road

Nearest station: Sandown, Simeon Path

Nearby places to visit: Dinosaur Isle; Wildheart Animal Sanctuary; National Poo Museum

❑ **Date visited:**
Notes on visit:

Skegness Pier

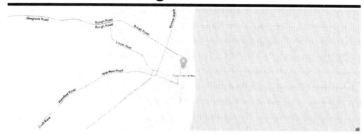

North Parade, PE25 2TE

Skegness Pier was opened in June 1881 and was the fourth longest pier in England at the time, stretching over 1,800 feet. Initially, it was a T-shaped pier that had a saloon and concert hall at the pier head. The pier was used for steamboat trips to Norfolk until 1910. During World War II, the pier was closed to prevent enemy invasion. In 1978, a severe storm caused significant damage to the pier, and the pier head and shelters were ultimately demolished in the mid-1980s due to high restoration costs. The pier has undergone various renovations in modern times, including redecking and waterproofing, allowing for year-round operation. The pier's main building also houses a bowling center, laser quest, and an indoor children's play centre. In early 2021, new owners announced their intentions to rebuild the pier to its original length of 1,909 feet.

Nearby pubs: Pier Beach Bar, Grand Parade; Wellies Bar, Grand Parade; The Jolly Fisherman, Grand Parade

Nearby cafes: The Beachside Tavern, Grand Parade; Charlies Shellfish Bar, Tower Esplanade; Seafood Cafe & Bar, Grand Parade

Nearby car parks: North Parade, Skegness; Scarbrough Esplanade, Skegness; Grand Parade, Skegness

Nearest bus stop: Scarborough Esplanade, North Parade

Nearest station: Skegness, Wainfleet Road

Nearby places to visit: Natureland Seal Sanctuary; The Village Church Farm

❏ **Date visited:**
Notes on visit:

43

Southampton: Royal Pier

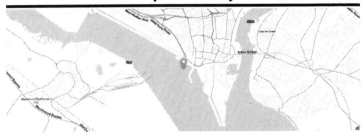

Town Quay, SO14 2AN

The Royal Pier, previously known as Victoria Pier, was built during the 1830s and served as a docking point for steamer services. Prior to its construction, steamer passengers had to navigate the muddy foreshore or use the overcrowded Town Quay. The pier was opened on 8 July 1833 by Princess Victoria, and was designed by Edward L Stephens, a Royal Navy officer. The foundations needing to be rebuilt in 1838. In 1871, a horse-drawn tramway was built to link the pier to Southampton Terminus railway station. The pier was rebuilt in iron over a two-year period starting in 1891, and the station was expanded to allow it to be used as a pleasure pier. The pier was reopened in 1902 by Prince Arthur, and was renamed Royal Pier. The pier was adapted to support RoRo ferries in the 1950s, and the pavilion was turned into a ballroom in 1963. The pier was closed in late 1979 and has remained in a state of disrepair since then, despite plans for redevelopment.

Nearby pubs: Dancing Man, Town Quay; Pig In The Wall, Western Esplanade; Duke of Wellington, 36 Bugle Street

Nearby cafes: Town Quay, St Mary's; Steam Coffee Shop, Town Quay; Steam Coffee Shop, Town Quay

Nearby car parks: Town Quay, St Mary's; Mayflower Roundabout, St Mary's; Herbert Walker Avenue, St Mary's

Nearest bus stop: Town Quay, St Mary's

Nearest station: Southampton Central, Blechynden Terrace

Nearby places to visit: Westquay; Ocean Village, Southampton; Medieval Merchant's House 🏛; Southampton Boat Show; Solent Sky; The Wool House; Southampton town walls; God's House Tower; Tudor House and Garden

❏ **Date visited:**
Notes on visit:

44

Southend Pier

Marine Parade, SS1 2ZG

Southend Pier stretches 2.16 kilometres (1.34 mi) into the Thames Estuary and holds the title of the longest pleasure pier in the world. The construction of the new pier, designed to replace a previous timber jetty, began in July 1829 following the Royal Assent in May 1829. In August 1889, the timber pier was substituted with an iron pier, and the Southend Pier Railway, the country's first pier railway, opened in the early 1890s. Throughout both world wars, the pier served various purposes, such as mooring ships housing German prisoners of war during World War I. In World War II, the Royal Navy commandeered the pier, renaming it HMS Leigh. After the war, around 6 million people visited the pier in 1949, and new attractions were introduced during the 1950s. However, a period of decline began in the 1970s due to structural deterioration, leading the council to announce closure plans in 1980. Following protests, the pier remained open, and a grant in 1983 allowed renovation work to take place, including the construction of a new pier railway opened by Princess Anne in 1986. The pier has experienced several fires, including those in 1959, 1976, 1995 and 2005. It is now a Grade II listed building.

Nearby pubs: Borough Hotel, 10-12 Marine Parade; Chinnery's, Marine Parade; The Royal, 1 High Street

Nearby cafes: Three Shells, Western Esplanade; High Street, Southchurch; SAVS Community Centre & Cafe, Alexandra Street

Nearby car parks: Marine Parade Bays, Jubilee Court; Seaway Car Park, Queensway; Royals, Chancellor Road

Nearest bus stop: Southend Pier, Western Esplanade

Nearest station: Shore, Marine Parade

Nearby places to visit: Adventure Island; Kursaal (amusement park)

❑ **Date visited:**
Notes on visit:

Southport Pier

Marine Drive, PR8 1RY

Southport Pier in Merseyside is a pleasure pier that first opened in August 1860. As the oldest iron pier in the country, it spans 1,108m (3,635 ft), making it the second-longest in Great Britain after Southend Pier. Although it once extended to 1,340m (4,380 ft), the pier's length was reduced in the late 19th and early 20th centuries due to a series of storms and fires. Renowned entertainers such as Charlie Chaplin have performed on the pier, and in its heyday it was frequented by steamliners. However, silting of the channel led to a decline in steamers visiting the pier by the 1920s, and the service ceased altogether in 1929. Throughout the late 20th century, the pier fell into disrepair and by 1990, it incurred significant annual losses alongside increasing maintenance costs. The local council attempted to have the pier demolished, but its efforts were thwarted by a single vote. Between 2000 and 2002, the pier underwent significant restoration and reopened to the public in May 2002. The Southport Pier Tramway, which ran from Southport Promenade to the pier head, operated at various times in the pier's history, most recently until June 2015. The pier is a Grade II listed building.

Nearby pubs: The Guelder Rose, Marine Drive; Brewers Fayre, Marine Parade; The Crown, Coronation Walk

Nearby cafes: Southport Pier Pavillion, Southport Pier; The Donut Hut, Southport Pier; Lakeside Cafe, Southport Pier

Nearby car parks: Marine Drive, Ocean Plaza Retail Park; Ocean Plaza Car Park, Southport Pier; Marine Drive, Southport

Nearest bus stop: Esplanade/Pleasureland, Esplanade

Nearest station: Southport Marine Parade, Marine Parade

Nearby places to visit: Pleasureland; Southport Zoo; Southport Model Railway Village

❑ **Date visited:**
Notes on visit:

46

Southsea: Clarence Pier

Long Curtain Road, PO5 3AX • www.clarencepier.co.uk

Clarence Pier is a well-known amusement pier located next to Southsea Hoverport. Unlike most seaside piers in the UK, it does not extend very far out to sea and instead goes along the coast. The pier was originally constructed in 1861 by the Prince and Princess of Wales and boasted a regular ferry service to the Isle of Wight. It was damaged by air raids during World War II and was reopened in its current form in 1961 after being rebuilt. The complex consists of a striking pavilion building with distinctive yellow and blue cladding and a small tower, with a fellow building next to it where the entrance to the rides is located. One of the main landmarks of Clarence Pier until the mid-1990s was the Super Loop ride, which has since been removed. The Ferris wheel was sold and relocated to Pleasureland Southport. The main building, known as the 'Golden Horseshoe', houses an amusement arcade as well as a small bowling alley. The Solent Wheel opened in Easter 2016 but was later taken down.

Nearby pubs: Brewers Fayre, Long Curtain Road; The Pembroke, 20 Pembroke Road; Dolphin, 41 High Street

Nearby cafes: Southsea Street Food, Long Curtain Road; Coffee Cup, Clarence Esplanade; Beach Bakery & Cakery, Clarence Esplanade

Nearby car parks: Long Curtain Road, Old Portsmouth; The Esplanade Car Park, Clarence Esplanade; Victoria Avenue, Old Portsmouth

Nearest bus stop: Clarence Pier Std A, Clarence Esplanade

Nearest station: Portsmouth Harbour, Phillip Avenue

Nearby places to visit: Domus Dei ▣; Southsea Castle; Spinnaker Tower; The D-Day Story; Portsmouth Cathedral; Haslar Marina; Royal Navy Submarine Museum; Round Tower (Portsmouth)

❑ **Date visited:**
Notes on visit:

Southsea: South Parade Pier

South Parade, PO4 0BW

The South Parade Pier was constructed in 1878 and officially opened to the public on 26 July 1879. It is one of two piers in the city of Portsmouth and has a long and eventful history. The pier once had a long hall down its centre that housed a seating area and a small restaurant. However, it fell into disrepair and was closed to the public in 2012 due to health and safety concerns. By 2017, the pier had been transformed into an amusement arcade and food outlet. It also contains a fishing deck and two function rooms that are often used for live music. In the summer of 2019, a funfair named Kidz Island was opened on the pier, and it has since become a popular attraction for families. The South Parade Pier has faced many challenges over the years, including a devastating fire during the filming of the movie Tommy in 1974.

Nearby pubs: The Gaiety Bar, Esplanade; The Beach Hut, South Parade; Coast Bar, St Helens Parade

Nearby cafes: Coffee @the Pier, South Parade; Rio Vitalise, South Parade; Baffled, Clarence Esplanade

Nearby car parks: Alhambra Road, Southsea; Mansion Road, Southsea; Rostrevor Lane, Southsea

Nearest bus stop: South Parade Pier, St Helens Parade

Nearest station: Fratton, Selbourne Terrace

Nearby places to visit: Southsea Castle; The D-Day Story; Portsmouth Pyramids Centre; The Wedgewood Rooms; Kings Theatre, Southsea

❏ **Date visited:**
Notes on visit:

Southwold Pier

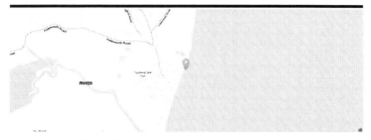

IP18 6EL • www.southwoldpier.co.uk

Southwold Pier, located in the coastal town of Southwold in Suffolk, England, extends 190 metres (620 ft) into the North Sea. It was originally built in 1900 as a landing stage for steamships carrying tourists from London to Clacton and Great Yarmouth until the 1930s. During the Second World War, the pier had a section removed due to the fear of its use during an invasion, and further damage occurred from an impact with a mine. The pier was rebuilt after the war at a cost of £30,000. The pier underwent major refurbishment in 1999 to rebuild it, which was completed in 2001, almost 100 years after it was first opened. In 2002, a new T-shaped end was added, bringing the pier to a total length of 208 yards (190 m). This additional length now allows the pier to accommodate visits by Britain's only surviving sea-going steam passenger ship, the PS Waverley paddle steamer and its running mate the MV Balmoral. Southwold Pier today is home to several shops and attractions, including traditional souvenir shops, cafés, restaurants and amusement arcades. It also includes a collection of modern coin-operated novelty machines designed and constructed by the inventor Tim Hunkin.

Nearby pubs: Sole Bay Inn, 7 East Green; The Lord Nelson, East Street; Red Lion, South Green

Nearby cafes: Cafe On The Green, Pier Avenue; The Clockhouse, Southwold Pier; Boating Lake Cafe, North Road

Nearby car parks: North Parade, Southwold; North Road, Southwold; Church Street, Southwold

Nearest bus stop: Pier, North Parade

Nearest station: Halesworth

Nearby places to visit: Southwold Lighthouse; Southwold Sailors' Reading Room

❏ **Date visited:**
Notes on visit:

49

Swanage Pier

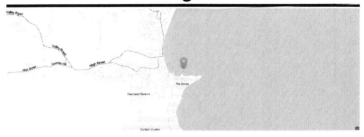

Swanage Pier, BH19 2AW

Swanage Pier was constructed in 1895 to provide passenger ship services and is situated on the eastern coast of the Isle of Purbeck. The first Swanage Pier was built between 1859 and 1860, measuring 750 feet long, for use primarily by the local stone quarrying industry. It included a tramway that ran the length of the pier and some way along the seafront. However, the old pier began to decline after the stone industry it served declined, leaving only its timber piles remaining today. When George Burt introduced regular steamer services between Swanage and nearby towns Poole and Bournemouth in 1874, a need arose for a second pier to be built primarily for passenger steamers. After steamer services discontinued in 1966, the remaining pleasure pier also began to fall into disrepair. In the 1990s, major restoration work was carried out on the pier's piles, timbers and ironwork fittings. Today small scale ferry services run daily throughout the summer season, mainly to Poole Quay. The pier also hosts a successful diving school, the oldest in the UK, and is visited annually by historic steamers including the Waverley paddle steamer. There is also a small aquarium showcasing the species of marine life found under the pier.

Nearby pubs: White Horse, High Street; Ship Inn, 23A; The White Swan, 31 High Street

Nearby cafes: The 1859 Swanage Pier, Swanage; Brook Tea Rooms, 15 The Parade; McAllisters, 24 Institute Road

Nearby car parks: Broad Road, Swanage; Broad Road Car Park, Broad Road; Peveril Point Road, Swanage

Nearest bus stop: Banjo Pier, Shore Road

Nearest station: Swanage, Railway Station Approach

Nearby places to visit: Swanage Museum & Heritage Centre

❏ **Date visited:**
Notes on visit:

Teignmouth: Grand Pier

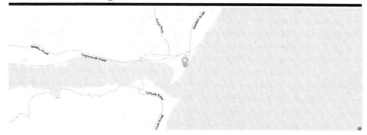

TQ14 8BD • www.teignmouthpier.com

The Grand Pier, also known as Teignmouth Pier, was designed by Joseph Wilson, an engineering consultant from London, and constructed between 1865 and 1867. The pier measures 212 metres (696 ft) in length and was initially built as a landing stage for steamboat passengers to get to the shore. The pier is constructed of cast-iron screw piles. During the Second World War, a section of the deck was removed to prevent the Germans from breaching England's coastal defenses. The Grand Pier was not brought back to its original width until the early 1960s. Visitors today can take a leisurely stroll along the pier and enjoy views of the coastline and the sea or spend time in the amusement arcade, cafes and restaurants located on the pier. It is now one of only two piers left on the south-west coast of England,

Nearby pubs: Teignmouth Social Club, Den Crescent; Rock Bottom, 9-10 Regent Street; Brass Monkey, Hollands Road

Nearby cafes: Beachcomber Cafe, Upper Den Carriageway; Luders Patisserie, Waterloo Street; Coasters, Triangle Place

Nearby car parks: Esplanade, The Street With No Name; Lower Brook Street, Teignmouth; Brunswick Street Car Park, Bath Terrace

Nearest bus stop: Teignmouth WH Smith Stop B, Lower Brook Street

Nearest station: Teignmouth, Higher Brook Street

Nearby places to visit:

❏ **Date visited:**
Notes on visit:

Torquay: Princess Pier

TQ2 5HA

Construction of Princess Pier began in 1890 with a simple groyne, followed by the addition of a steel and timber structure in 1894 and a landing quay on the seaward side of the pier-head in 1906. A modern shelter was built in 1965. In 1974, a fire destroyed 'The Islander' entertainment building on the pier-head and revealed severe corrosion in the steel superstructure, requiring urgent repairs. In February 2014, the pier was closed indefinitely due to severe damage caused by powerful waves that lifted concrete and exposed electricity cables; repair work was completed in 2016. A major refurbishment project began the following year. In May 2022, a fire destroyed a nearby superyacht, delaying further repairs to the pier. It has since reopened. (Torquay also has a working pier, Haldon Pier, built in 1867 as a breakwater alongside the harbour.)

Nearby pubs: Visto Lounge, A379 Upton; Appleby's, Shedden Hill Road; Vaughans, Vaughan Parade

Nearby cafes: Breezes, Torbay Road; Costa Coffee, A379 Upton; WeSup, Palk Street

Nearby car parks: Torbay Road, Upton; Torbay Road, Ellacombe; Warren Road, Upton

Nearest bus stop: Princess Theatre, Torbay Road

Nearest station: Torquay, Rathmore Road

Nearby places to visit: Torre Abbey; Living Coasts; Torquay Museum

❏ **Date visited:**
Notes on visit:

Totland Bay: Totland Pier

Madeira Road, PO39 0JP

Totland Bay is a quarter of a mile (0.4 km) west of the village of Totland on the Isle of Wight. It has 450-foot-long (140 m) Victorian pier, which was completed in March 1880, replacing a previous wooden structure. It offered facilities such as a pier-head shelter and a small amusement pavilion. A ferry service ceased at the end of the 1927 summer season, but pleasure cruises continued until 1931. The pier was sectioned during World War II for defense measures and was then repaired. It reopened in 1951, with a new pier-head shelter constructed in the 1950s. The National Physical Laboratory installed a data gathering centre here in 1975; the pier has changed owners several times since, and was later left derelict. In 2022 further renovation work included creating a new restaurant, although in early 2023 it was reported this could be replaced by holiday rental property.

Nearby pubs: Highdown Inn, Highdown Lane; The Vine, 1 School Green Road; The Wight Horsebox Bar, Alum Bay New Road

Nearby cafes: Bay Cafe, Madeira Road; Dawnie's Coffee House, The Broadway; Longbeach Bar, Colwell Chine Road

Nearby car parks: Madeira Road, Middleton; Esplanade Walk, Middleton; Granville Road, Middleton

Nearest bus stop: Totland, War Memorial

Nearest station: Lymington Pier, South Baddesley Road (mainland via ferry)

Nearby places to visit: Widdick Chine, Yarmouth Castle

❏ **Date visited:**

Notes on visit:

Walton-on-the-Naze: Walton Pier

Marine Parade, BS21 7QS

Walton Pier, one of the earliest in the country, was originally built in 1830 with a length of 150 ft for landing goods and passengers on steamers to Walton. It was extended to 330 ft in 1848, but was badly damaged in a storm in January 1871. A second pier opened in 1880 but also did not last. In 1895, the Walton Pier & Hotel Company Ltd opened a replacement pier 500 ft longer than the original, and in 1898 it was extended to 2610 ft, making it the third longest pier in the country. When the new pier opened in 1895, an electric tramway was installed to transport passengers from the steamers to the front of the pier, and was in use until 1935 when it was upgraded to a battery-powered carriage. In 1937, the pier was bought by Charles Goss, who established a pavilion at the seaward end, an amusement arcade, a tent that served as a theatre, and the Seaspray Lounge. In 1945, fire damaged the pier and the tramway carriage was replaced by a diesel locomotive, removed in the 1970s. In February 2021, part of the pier collapsed into the sea during Storm Darcy. In 2022, the pier underwent a major revamp with a large arcade area,. The Walton and Frinton lifeboat has been moored afloat near the end of the pier since 1900.

Nearby pubs: Moon and Sixpence, 15 The Beach; The Royal Oak, 35 Copse Road; The Little Harp Inn, Elton Road

Nearby cafes: Pagoda Tea Room, Marine Parade; Hut Café, Alexandra Road; Scarletts, 20 The Beach

Nearby car parks: Beach Mews, Walton Park; Elton Road, West End; Burden Park, West End

Nearest bus stop: Elton Road, West End

Nearest station: Yatton, Station Approach

Nearby places to visit: Clevedon Pier; Curzon Community Cinema, Clevedon

❏ **Date visited:**
Notes on visit:

Weston-super-Mare: Birnbeck Pier

Birkett Road, BS23 2ER

Birnbeck Pier, also known as the 'Old Pier', is situated on the Bristol Channel. It is the only pier in the country that links the mainland to an island, connecting to Birnbeck Island. The Grade II* listed pier was designed by Eugenius Birch and opened in 1867, making it one of only six Grade II* piers surviving in the country. The refreshment and waiting rooms were designed in 1898 by local architect Hans Price. The pier has been closed to the public since 1994 and is now on the Buildings at Risk Register. During the late 19th and early 20th centuries, the pier was popular with both locals and tourists and served as a boarding point for steamers in the Bristol Channel and underwent various modifications over the years. During the Second World War, the pier was commissioned as HMS Birnbeck by the Admiralty as part of a weapons research facility. The pier reopened after the war, but the number of visitors and steamer passengers declined, with the final excursion visiting the pier in 1979. Since its closure, ownership has changed many times, and it has been subject to a series of unsuccessful proposals for its redevelopment. The pier has remained in a largely derelict state, with part of it collapsing during storms at the end of 2015.

Nearby pubs: Cove, Birnbeck Road; The Criterion, 45 Upper Church Road; The Regency, Lower Church Road

Nearby cafes: Cafe La Mer, 22 West Street; The Green House Café, Royal Parade; Grove Lane, Weston-super-Mare

Nearby car parks: Birkett Road, Weston-super-Mare; Knightstone Causeway, Weston-super-Mare; Knightstone Road, Weston-super-Mare

Nearest bus stop: Birnbeck Pier, Birkett Road

Nearest station: Weston-super-Mare, Station Approach

Nearby places to visit: Grand Pier, Weston-super-Mare

❏ **Date visited:**
Notes on visit:

Weston-super-Mare: Grand Pier

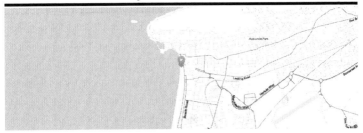

Promenade, BS23 1AL • www.grandpier.co.uk

The Grand Pier is a popular pleasure pier situated on the Bristol Channel. It was opened in 1904 and has been a Grade II listed building since 1983. The pier is 366 metres (1,201 ft) long and is one of two major piers in the town, along with the now derelict Birnbeck Pier. At the end of the pier wen it was built was a 2,000-seat theatre used for music halls, opera, stage plays and ballet. An extension measuring 500 yards (1,500 ft) was opened in May 1907, with the intention that the pier would be used as a docking point for boats to Cardiff. However, the dangerous currents in the bay made this too difficult, and the extension was later demolished. The pier's pavilion has been destroyed by fire on two occasions, in 1930 and 2008. The theatre at the pier's end was destroyed by fire in 1930. The replacement pavilion housed a large undercover funfair rather than a theatre. In 2008, a fire at the foot of the north tower on the shoreward (eastern) end of the pavilion destroyed the building; a new pavilion opened in 2010, costing £39,000,000. The pier was officially reopened in 2011 by Princess Anne.

Nearby pubs: Ella's Bar, Parade Park, Yates's, York Street; Dragon Kiss, 18-20 Regent Street

Nearby cafes: Beach Cafe, Marine Parade; Victorian Cafe, Promenade; Brunello Lounge, 4-5 Beach Road

Nearby car parks: Saint Margaret's Terrace, Weston-super-Mare; Salisbury Terrace, Weston-super-Mare; Italian Gardens, Weston-super-Mare

Nearest bus stop: Winter Gardens (k), Promenade

Nearest station: Weston-super-Mare, Station Approach

Nearby places to visit: Lambretta Scooter Museum; Weston Museum; Dismaland

❏ **Date visited:**
Notes on visit:

Weymouth: Pier Bandstand

Esplanade, DT4 7RN

The Pier Bandstand Weymouth is a stunning art deco structure located on the shore of Weymouth Bay. Built between 1938 and 1939, the bandstand was designed by V J Wenning, who won the architectural competition for its design. It was officially opened in 1939. It is made up of 3,050 metric tons of concrete, 180 metric tons of steel, 750 metres of neon tubing, and 1,200 light bulbs. The Pier Bandstand was designed with the bandstand extending out into the sea from a two-storey building adjoining the promenade. The seaward section was able to seat 2,400 people. Despite criticism for its visual impact along the bay, it quickly became a popular attraction and was used to host many events, from dances and concerts to wrestling and roller skating. However, in the 1980s, the seaward end of the bandstand was in need of major repair, and it was cheaper to demolish the bandstand and only the landward building was left standing. Today, the Pier Bandstand houses the Italian restaurant Al Molo, along with an amusement arcade and gift shop within its ground-level kiosks.

Nearby pubs: The Waterloo, 1 Grange Road; The Park, Carlton Road South; Railway Tavern, 6 Queen Street

Nearby cafes: Hamiltons Cafe, 5 Brunswick Terrace; Aunt Vi's Tea and Cake, Esplanade; Cafe123 123 The Esplanade, Melcombe Regis

Nearby car parks: Melcombe Avenue, Melcombe Regis; Upway Street, Melcombe Regis; Gloucester Mews, Rodwell

Nearest bus stop: Westerhall, Dorchester Road

Nearest station: Weymouth, Ranelagh Road

Nearby places to visit: Nothe Fort; Weymouth Beach; Weymouth Pavilion; Weymouth Marina; Weymouth Harbour Tramway; Weymouth Harbour

❏ **Date visited:**

Notes on visit:

Weymouth Pier

The Esplanade, DT4 8EA

The history of Weymouth Pier dates back to 1812, though there is little documented evidence of its origins. The current pier was constructed in reinforced concrete and opened in 1933, costing £120,000. It measures 400 metres in length and varies between 30 metres in width at the shoreward end and 12 metres at the seaward end. The pier was divided into two halves when built; the southern side was reserved for commercial use and was equipped to load and unload cargo from harbour ships. he northern side was fenced off from the industrial section and was a promenade area, which included shelters, a diving stage, changing rooms, and an illuminated view of Weymouth Bay and Nothe Fort at night. Over the years, the pier has undergone several renovations and reconstructions. In 1860, the pier was largely rebuilt in timber and extended to a length of 273 metres. A cargo stage was added in 1877, and a landing stage and baggage handling hall were built in 1889. The Weymouth Pavilion opened in 1908, and the pier was rebuilt in the 1930s. The Ritz Theatre, renamed after the war, was destroyed in a fire in 1954, and a new Pavilion opened in 1961. The pier was widened in 1971-1972 to create a new ferry terminal. A 2012 addition was the Weymouth Sea Life Tower.

Nearby pubs: The Nothe Tavern, Barrack Road; The Cutter, 4 East Street; TJ's Steakasaurus Eatery & Bar, Custom House Quay

Nearby cafes: Stone Pier Cafe, Barrack Road; The Nothe Cafe, Barrack Road; The Boat Beach Cafe, Esplanade

Nearby car parks: Pavilion, The Esplanade; Barrack Road, Rodwell; Barrack Road, Rodwell

Nearest bus stop: King's Statue (K5), Esplanade

Nearest station: Weymouth, Ranelagh Road

Nearby places to visit: Nothe Fort; Weymouth Beach; Weymouth Pavilion

❏ **Date visited:**
Notes on visit:

Worthing Pier

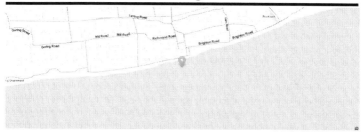

Marine Parade, BN11 3QA

Worthing Pier has been open to the public since its opening by Sir Robert Rawlinson on 12 April 1862. Originally constructed as a simple promenade deck that was 960 ft (290 m) long and 15 ft (4.6 m) wide, the pier was later upgraded in 1888. The width of the pier was increased to 30 ft (9.1 m) and the pier head was increased to 105 ft (32 m) to accommodate a 650-seat pavilion. The pier was later named a Grade II listed building structure. The pier has a rich history, having been the site of the first moving picture show in Worthing in 1896. In March 1913, the pier was damaged in a storm, leaving only the southern end remaining, which was affectionately named 'Easter Island'. A rebuilt pier was opened in 1914. The pier has also seen its share of destruction, with all but the northern pavilion being destroyed in a fire in September 1933. The pier was sectioned in 1940 for fear of German invasion after the British retreat at Dunkirk, with army engineers using explosives to blow a 120ft hole in the pier to prevent it from being used as a landing stage. Today, the pier features a Pavilion Theatre and Denton Cafe at the northern end, a 1935 amusement arcade in the middle, and a tearoom and function area at the southern end.

Nearby pubs: Slicks, Marine Parade; The Projectionist's Bar, Marine Parade; Bar 42 42 Marine Parade, West Worthing

Nearby cafes: Son of a Peach, Marine Parade; The Cow Shed, 31A; Munch, 3-5 Royal Arcade

Nearby car parks: Montague Place, Worthing; Level 1 Worthing, West Sussex; Chatsworth Road, Worthing

Nearest bus stop: Marine Parade, Worthing

Nearest station: Worthing, Railway Approach

Nearby places to visit: Worthing Museum and Art Gallery

❑ **Date visited:**
Notes on visit:

Yarmouth Pier

Pier Street, PO41 0NJ

Yarmouth Pier, built during the Victorian era, is the longest wooden pier in England, measuring 186 metres in length. It opened in 1876 and was damaged by a ship only weeks later. New offices and a waiting room were built in 1927 for passengers travelling by ferry to Lymington's railway on the mainland. The pier has undergone several restoration schemes due to the relatively short lifespan of the wooden piles used in its construction. In 2008, it reopened to the public following its latest restoration scheme. The pier's historical significance is evident in its ornate architecture. Its unique design features a covered walkway built in the 1980s, which allows visitors to enjoy a stroll along its length regardless of the weather. Additionally, the pier's location offers breathtaking views of the Isle of Wight coastline, making it an ideal spot for photography and sightseeing.

Nearby pubs: The George Hotel, Quay Street; Bugle Coaching Inn, Market Square; The King's Head, Quay Street

Nearby cafes: The Gossips Café, Pier Street; PO41 Coffee House, Quay Street; Castle Café, Quay Street

Nearby car parks: Pier Street, Yarmouth; High Street, Yarmouth; Market Square, Yarmouth

Nearest bus stop: Yarmouth, Bus Station

Nearest station: Lymington Pier, South Baddesley Road

Nearby places to visit: Yarmouth Castle ▣

❑ **Date visited:**
Notes on visit:

60

PIERS IN WALES

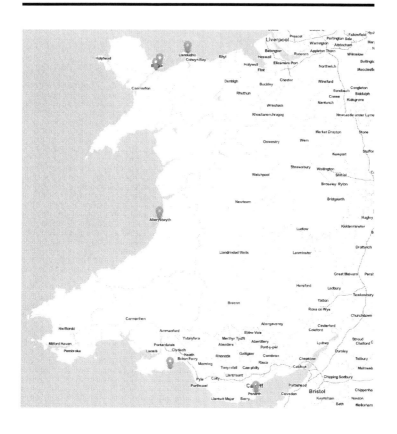

Aberystwyth: Royal Pier

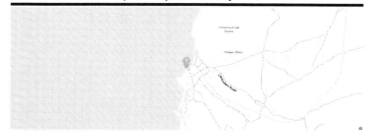

Rhodfa Newydd / New Promenade, SY23 2AZ

The Royal Pier opened on Good Friday in 1865, coinciding with the opening of the Cambrian Railways line from Machynlleth, and was the first in Wales. Over the years, the pier has experienced significant damage from a series of heavy storms, resulting in its current much shorter length compared to its original 242 metres (794 ft). The Aberystwyth Pier Promenade Company commissioned the construction of the pier and it was designed and built by renowned pier engineer Eugenius Birch. Its structure featured iron rod braces, cast iron piles, and supporting columns concreted into the rock. A severe storm in January 1866 destroyed a 30-metre (98 ft) section at the pier's seaward end but the damaged section was replaced by new owners in the 1870s. A glass pavilion was later constructed at the landward end, opening in 1896. In 1938 a storm destroyed the promenade and 200 feet (61 m) of the pier. The pier remained closed during World War II, as its deteriorating state made repairing it a security risk. It was closed again in the 1970s but the remaining 91 metres (299 ft) of the structure were repaired in 1986. A snooker hall and restaurant were opened in a refurbished pavilion in 1987.

Nearby pubs: Inn on the Pier, Glan y Môr / Marine Terrace; The Pier Hotel, 33 Heol y Wig / Pier Street; Downies Vaults, 33 Y Porth Bach / Eastgate

Nearby cafes: The Cabin / Y Caban, 21A-21B; Starbucks, 47-49 Y Stryd Fawr / Great Darkgate Street; Agnelli's, 3 Heol y Bont / Bridge Street

Nearby car parks: Rhodfa Newydd / New Promenade, Aberystwyth; Glan y Môr / Marine Terrace, Aberystwyth; Stryd Y Brenin / King Street, Aberystwyth

Nearest bus stop: Royal Pier, Glan y Môr / Marine Terrace

Nearest station: Aberystwyth, Ffordd Alexandra / Alexandra Road

Nearby places to visit: Aberystwyth Cliff Railway; Vale of Rheidol Railway

❏ **Date visited:**
Notes on visit:

Bangor: Garth Pier

Bangor Pier, LL57 2SU

Garth Pier, also known as Bangor Pier, is a Grade II listed structure. Spanning 1,500 feet (460 m) in length, it is recognized as the second-longest pier in Wales and the ninth longest in the British Isles. The pier was designed by J.J. Webster of Westminster, London, and features cast-iron columns with a steel structure, including the handrails. The wooden deck of the pier is adorned with a series of octagonal kiosks with roofs, street lighting, and a pontoon landing stage for pleasure steamers on the Menai Strait. The pier officially opened to the public on 14 May 1896. Throughout its history, the pier has faced several challenges, including damage, threats of demolition, and restoration efforts. In August 2017, it was announced that major restoration work would take place at a cost of £1 million, as the pier had not received any significant maintenance in many years. The pier head reopened to the public in 2021. The pier has also become a haven for local seabirds due to its location and length, allowing close viewing of various bird species. Today, the pier's kiosks house small cafes, artist studios, and a shop supplying crabbing and fishing gear.

Nearby pubs: Tap & Spile, 83 Lower Garth Road; Ship Launch, Lower Garth Road; The Boatyard, Lower Garth Road

Nearby cafes: Whistlestop Café, Garth Road; The Pavilion, Bangor Pier; Joy's Café, 27 Stryd Y Deon

Nearby car parks: Bangor Pier, Garth; Ffordd Siliwen, Garth; Lower Garth Road, Garth

Nearest bus stop: Garth Road, Garth

Nearest station: Bangor, Holyhead Road

Nearby places to visit: Storiel (museum and gallery); Bangor Cathedral

❑ **Date visited:**
Notes on visit:

Beaumaris Pier

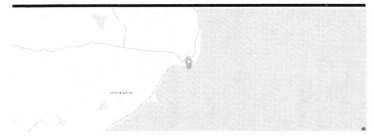

B5109, LL58 8BS

Beaumaris Pier on Anglesey was initially designed by Frederick Foster and opened in 1846. The pier featured a concrete and stone neck, wooden piles supporting iron girders, and a wooden deck. It was later rebuilt in 1872 following the new classical Victorian era civil engineering lines, boasting screw piles made from iron, steel supporting girders, and again a wooden deck. In 1895, the deck length was extended to 570 feet (170 m), and a T-shaped pontoon end, a pavilion, and a 2 ft 6 in (762 mm) railway baggage line were added. The reconstruction was undertaken to attract the pleasure steamers of the Liverpool and North Wales Steamship Company, which sailed between Liverpool, Llandudno and the Isle of Man along the Menai Strait. However, the popularity of pleasure steamer services began to decline before World War II due to competition from cheaper motor buses. This decline led to the decision to demolish the T-head pontoon. In the 1960s, the pier became unsafe due to lack of maintenance and faced the threat of demolition. However, a large private donation from local yachtswoman and RNLI lifeboat secretary Miss Mary Burton saved the pier.

Nearby pubs: The George and Dragon, Heol yr Eglwys / Church Street; The Bold Arms, Heol yr Eglwys / Church Street; Liverpool Arms, 56 Castle Street

Nearby cafes: Beau's Tea Room, 30 Heol y Castell / Castle Street; Jolly's Coffee House & Patisserie, 5 Heol y Castell / Castle Street; Happy Valley Pavilion Cafe, Castle Street

Nearby car parks: Heol Victoria Street, Beaumaris; B5109 Beaumaris, Ynys Môn / Isle of Anglesey; Heol Alma Street, Beaumaris

Nearest bus stop: Heol y Castell / Castle Street, Beaumaris

Nearest station: Bangor, Holyhead Road

Nearby places to visit: Beaumaris Castle 🏰; Beaumaris Gaol

❏ **Date visited:**
Notes on visit:

Llandudno Pier

Happy Valley Road, LL30 2QL

Llandudno Pier is a historic Grade II* listed structure which spans 2,295 feet (700 metres); it is the longest pier in Wales and the fifth longest in England and Wales. The pier features a deep-water landing stage at its end, which has been completely rebuilt three times, most recently in 1969. This landing stage was once used by the Isle of Man Steam Packet Company for occasional excursions to Douglas, Isle of Man, and for the annual visit of preserved steamers PS Waverley or MV Balmoral. Llandudno Pier is unique for having two entrances: one on the promenade at North Parade and the other on Happy Valley Road, which is no longer in use. The Grand Hotel is located between the two entrances. The pier's origins date back to a shorter, 242-foot (74-meter) structure built on 16 wooden piles in 1858 by the St. George's Harbour and Railway Company. However, this original pier was severely damaged in the Royal Charter Storm of 1859 and was subsequently deemed too short for practical use. Today, the landing stage is no longer utilized for steamers but serves as a platform for anglers to fish off the end of the pier, and it is not accessible to the general public.

Nearby pubs: Oceans Bar, North Parade; Snooze, 3 Church Walks; The Baytree Hotel, North Parade

Nearby cafes: Oceans Cafe, Happy Valley Road; Happy Valley Cafe (Parisellas), Happy Valley Walks; Llandudno Pier Coffee Shop, North Parade

Nearby car parks: Happy Valley Road, Craig-y-don; Marine Drive, Craig-y-don; Happy Valley Walks, Craig-y-don

Nearest bus stop: North Parade, Llandudno

Nearest station: Llandudno, Jubilee Street

Nearby places to visit: Venue Cymru; Llandudno Cable Car

❑ **Date visited:**
Notes on visit:

Mumbles Pier

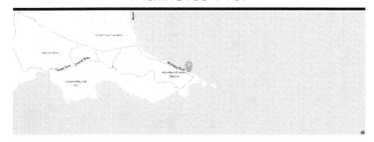

ILB Slipway, SA3 4EN

The Grade II listed Mumbles Pier is a 255-metre (835 feet) long Victorian pleasure pier that was constructed in 1898. Situated at the south-western corner of Swansea Bay, it falls within the city of Swansea. The pier was designed by W. Sutcliffe Marsh and promoted by John Jones Jenkins of the Rhondda and Swansea Bay Railway. It opened on 10 May 1898 at a cost of £10,000 and was the western terminus for the world's first passenger-carrying horsecar railway, the Swansea and Mumbles Railway. Additionally, the pier served as a major terminal for the White Funnel paddle steamers of P & A Campbell, unloading tourists from routes along the River Severn and Bristol Channel. During World War II, the pier was requisitioned. A new arcade was built on the pier's frontage in 1966. By the early 21st century, the pier had fallen into a state of disrepair, with a large section fenced off to visitors and other areas patched up to maintain safety. During a major renovation in 2012, a new lifeboat station and RNLI gift shop were built at the end of the pier, with fishing platforms added. Today, the pier is used for fishing and tourism, offering panoramic views of Swansea Bay, and there is an entertainment complex at the base of the pier.

Nearby pubs: The Pilot, 726 Mumbles Road; The George, 706 Mumbles Road; Ty Cwrw, Mumbles Road

Nearby cafes: Mumbles Pier Beach Hut Cafe, Mumbles Road; The Shared Plate, 646 Mumbles Road; Ponderosa, 626 Mumbles Road

Nearby car parks: Mumbles Road, Thistleboon; Mumbles Head Car Park, Mumbles Road; Bracelet Bay Car Park, Mumbles Road

Nearest bus stop: Pier Hotel (NE), Mumbles Road

Nearest station: Swansea, Strand Ringmore

Nearby places to visit: Langland Bay

❏ **Date visited:**
Notes on visit:

Penarth Pier

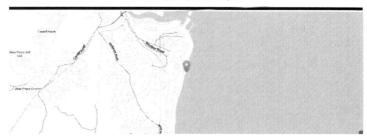

Beach Road, CF64 3AU

Penarth Pier opened its doors in 1898, after earlier unsuccessful attempts to build a pier here connected to a ferry service to Cardiff. It has attracted many seaside-goers who also enjoyed the pleasure steamers that operated from the pier. Over the years, Penarth Pier has experienced several instances of vessels colliding with the structure and a fire breaking out in one of the pavilions in 1931. While the wooden pavilion was never replaced, a concrete pavilion has been utilized for various purposes such as a concert hall, ballroom and cinema. Today, the Penarth Pier Pavilion resides in this concrete structure. The pier is 750 feet (230 m) long.

Nearby pubs: Railway Hotel, 1 Plymouth Road; Crafty Devil, 17 Windsor Road; Saint Fagan's Castle, 114 Glebe Street

Nearby cafes: Decks Takeaway, The Esplanade; Coffi Co, The Esplanade; Pickford's Galley and Bar with Rooms, The Esplanade

Nearby car parks: Rectory Road, Morristown; Rectory Road Lane, Morristown; Berkley Drive, Morristown

Nearest bus stop: Penarth Pier NE, Beach Road

Nearest station: Penarth, Station Approach

Nearby places to visit: Turner House Gallery

❏ **Date visited:**
Notes on visit:

PIERS IN SCOTLAND

Dunoon Pier

Pier Esplanade, PA23 7HJ

Dunoon Pier extends into the Firth of Clyde. Although completed in its current form in 1898, its earliest parts can be traced back to 1835. Today, the pier is classified as a Category A listed structure, and is regarded as the finest surviving example of a timber ferry pier in the country. A more robust structure was built in 1841 due to increased tourism in the town. However, this second version was destroyed in a storm just three years later. It was reconstructed the next year and extended in 1867 by Campbell Douglas. In 1868, James Hunter of Hafton House bought the pier and made significant enlargements, adding conveniences for both passenger and goods traffic. The pier once hosted a ferry service to the Cloch Lighthouse. The pier was extended to its current structure between 1896 and 1898. In 2005, it was shortened to accommodate the construction of a breakwater to the south of the pier, which aimed to protect the pier's architecture from storm surges. In addition to the breakwater, a new link span was installed to allow the berthing of roll-on/roll-off ferries. Argyll and Bute Council partially refurbished the pier in 2015, and it now serves purely as a tourist attraction.

Nearby pubs: The Osborne, 44 Shore Road; The Villager Royal, Pier Road; Station Bar, Row 12 (HGV)

Nearby cafes: Rock Cafe, Pier Esplanade; Argyll Street, Auchamore; Yachtsman Cafe, Victoria Parade

Nearby car parks: Argyll Street, Auchamore; A815 Bogleha, Dunoon; Moir Street Car Park, Moir Street

Nearest bus stop: Dunoon Ferry Terminal (Stop 3), Pier Esplanade

Nearest station: Inverkip, Station Avenue

Nearby places to visit: Castle House Museum

❏ **Date visited:**
Notes on visit:

Fort William Town Pier

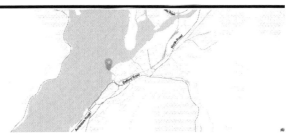

A82, PH33 6DB

In 1894, the West Highland Railway commenced operations, with Fort William as its primary hub. MacBrayne's steamers docked at the pier, just a short distance from the old station. Besides steamers, buses connected the pier and station. The original station no longer exists and has been replaced by the A82 dual carriageway, with Fort William's new station situated to the north-east. Fort William Town Pier is now home to Crannog Seafood Restaurant. In 1989, local fisherman Finlay Finlayson transformed a bait shed on the town pier into the restaurant, allowing him to serve his catch directly to patrons. Crannog also offers cruises down Loch Linnhe, departing from the pier, where tourists can enjoy extensive views and local wildlife.

Nearby pubs: The Great Glen, 98-104 High Street; Ben Nevis, 103 High Street; Grog and Gruel, 66 High Street

Nearby cafes: The Hot Roast Company, 127 High Street; Café 115 115117 High Street, Plantation; Costa, 102-104 High Street

Nearby car parks: A861 Trislaig, Ardgour; West End Car Park, Achintore Road; A82 An Aird, Fort William

Nearest bus stop: Pier, A861 Trislaig

Nearest station: Corpach, Road to the Isles

Nearby places to visit: West Highland Museum

❑ **Date visited:**
Notes on visit:

Helensburgh Pier

Pier Road, G84 8RQ

Helensburgh Pier, stretching 245 metres from the coast with a depth of 2.2 metres off the pier head, is a stone-built pier with a timber extension. The pier has suffered from little maintenance, causing the timber extension to deteriorate significantly. Previously, the pier was used by infrequent small boats and the Waverley steamer during its annual summer sailing schedule in the Clyde, which has now ceased. The pier has a rich history, dating back to 1816 when Henry Bell, the former Provost of Helensburgh and inventor of The Comet, built the first pier in the town. The pier's design is largely attributed to William Spence in 1859, with the timber extension added in 1871. In recent years concerns have been raised about the deteriorating condition of the pier. After a fire around the turn of the century, a significant portion of the pier had been left to decay, and the remaining structure required urgent conservation work. In June 2019, the pier was designated as a Category C listed structure by Historic Environment Scotland (HES) for its rarity as a surviving 19th-century stone and timber former steamer pier and its historical relationship with the town. In 2022, funding was approved for pier improvement work as part of a wider area regeneration package.

Nearby pubs: Rhu Inn, Gareloch Road; Ardencaple, Gareloch Road; The Commodore, 112-117 West Clyde Street

Nearby cafes: Cafe Rhu, Gareloch Road; The Beachcomber, Rhu Road Lower; The Coffee Club, Colquhoun Square

Nearby car parks: Gareloch Road, Rhu; Gareloch Road, Rhu; Torwoodhill Road, Rhu

Nearest bus stop: Gareloch Road, Rhu

Nearest station: Helensburgh Upper, West Rossdhu Drive

Nearby places to visit: The Hill House; Hermitage Park; Scottish Submarine Centre

❏ **Date visited:**

Notes on visit:

Kilcreggan Pier

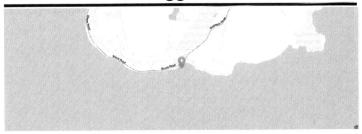

Shore Road, G84 oJJ

Kilcreggan overlooks the Clyde estuary towards Gourock and Greenock. The original pier was built in 1850 and replaced by the current pier in 1897. At that time, nearly 40 steamers would call at Kilcreggan daily, transporting passengers to various destinations including Glasgow and Rothesay. The B-listed structure was strengthened in 1964, when the present pierhead building was added. Nowadays, the pier primarily serves the CalMac ferry link with Gourock and the Waverley, which calls twice a week during its summer season. A passenger ferry also operates to Gourock regularly, and makes additional stops at Helensburgh during the summer months. As the region's last traditional wooden pier in daily use, it is a unique survivor of the Clyde steamers' heyday. Despite challenges, the pier has endured, but its future is uncertain, as Argyll and Bute Council has estimated that millions may need to be spent on a new pontoon and breakwater.

Nearby pubs: Cleats, Kempock Street; Cafe Continental, Lower Kempock Street; The Kempock Bar, Kempock Street

Nearby cafes: Bakehouse, Kempock Street; Fresh, Kempock Street; Good Brew, Kempock Street

Nearby car parks: Shore Road, Kilcreggan; Shore Road, Peaton; Fort Road, Kilcreggan

Nearest bus stop: Lower Kempock Street, Midton

Nearest station: Gourock, Station Road

Nearby places to visit: Cove Burgh Hall; McLean Museum (Greenock)

❏ **Date visited:**
Notes on visit:

74

Rothesay Pier

Pier Lane, PA20 0LH

Rothesay is on the Isle of Bute, located in the Firth of Clyde. Its original masonry pier of traditional construction was established in 1752 and completed in 1781, but was replaced by a wooden pier in the Victorian era when the town experienced its heyday, the pier bustling with ferries carrying tourists from Glasgow. Rothesay Pier was the centre of steamer traffic, featuring an elegant Scottish Baronial terminal building that unfortunately burned down in 1962. By the late 1800s, the journey from Glasgow, once taking days, was reduced to a mere two-hour steamer trip. In 1913, steamers made 100 calls at Rothesay, and the town's summer population swelled to 50,000 people. Rothesay's popularity continued through the inter-war years but declined in later decades due to the emergence of affordable package holidays abroad. Today, only a cabbie's shelter and public toilets remain of Rothesay Pier's 1903 buildings, with the latter being especially noteworthy for its tiled walls, black marble mosaic floors, and burnished copper piping. The current terminal, built in 1992, echoes the design of the first pier with its pagoda roof and red tiles. The new Rothesay Pier and Harbour redevelopment was opened in 2009.

Nearby pubs: Anchor Bar, 36 Marine Road; The Port Inn, 45 Marine Road; Mac's Bar, 14 Castlehill Street

Nearby cafes: CaleDonia Coffeehouse & Bistro, 31 Marine Road; Port Bannatyne Post Office, 46 Marine Road; Zavaroni's, Argyle Street

Nearby car parks: Argyle Place, Rothesay; Chapel Hill Road, Rothesay; West Peir, Rothesay

Nearest bus stop: High Road, Port Bannatyne

Nearest station: N/A

Nearby places to visit: Rothesay Castle

❏ **Date visited:**
Notes on visit:

Printed in Great Britain
by Amazon

22465313R00044